PHILIP GEARING is Professor of Vocational and Adult Education at the University of North Florida in Jacksonville. He is also the author of the three-volume work, *English for Adults* and the six-volume *General Education Series* (English, Science, Social Studies, Literature, Mathematics, and Review). EVELYN BRUNSON is Associate Professor of Business Teacher Education at the University of North Florida, Jacksonville and is the author of *The Professional Secretary.*

PHILIP J. GEARING
EVELYN V. BRUNSON

BREAKING INTO PRINT

How to Get Your Work Published

A SPECTRUM BOOK

PRENTICE-HALL, INC., Englewood Cliffs, New Jersey 07632

Library of Congress Cataloging in Publication Data

Gearing, Philip J
  Breaking into print.

  (A Spectrum Book)
  Includes index.
  1. Authorship.   2. Authors and publishers.   I. Brunson,
  Evelyn V., date   joint author.   II. Title.
  PN155.G4   808'.02   77-477
  ISBN 0-13-081687-6
  ISBN 0-13-081679-5 pbk.

This book is dedicated to *you*, the reader.

© 1977 by Prentice-Hall, Inc., Englewood Cliffs, N.J. 07632

A Spectrum Book

Printed in the United States of America

10   9   8   7   6   5   4   3

PRENTICE-HALL INTERNATIONAL, INC., *London*
PRENTICE-HALL OF AUSTRALIA PTY. LIMITED, *Sydney*
PRENTICE-HALL OF CANADA, LTD., *Toronto*
PRENTICE-HALL OF INDIA PRIVATE LIMITED, *New Delhi*
PRENTICE-HALL OF JAPAN, INC., *Tokyo*
PRENTICE-HALL OF SOUTHEAST ASIA PTE. LTD., *Singapore*
WHITEHALL BOOKS LIMITED, *Wellington, New Zealand*

Contents

Preface

This book has been written with YOU in mind! Having struggled through the throes of publications of various kinds, the authors have learned through experience . . . the hard way. We hope to make the path a little easier for you.

There are thousands of aspiring authors out there . . . somewhere . . . who, with a little guidance, might become successfully published. We cannot guarantee to develop a professional author out of everyone, but if you follow the advice given in this book, you at will least know how to approach a publisher and what will be expected before publication.

We tell you

. . . how to start
   . . . how to find a publisher
      . . . how to negotiate a contract

. . . how to prepare copy
   . . . how to plan for spending royalties.

We also provide

. . . evaluative criteria

to help you in maintaining writing quality. What more can you ask? (Turn to the Contents, and you'll probably find it!)
This book is prepared to help authors in all fields . . .

from sexy novels . . .
   to children's books . . .
      to textbooks in all areas . . .

from professional journals . . .
   to short stories for popular household magazines . . .

from poems . . .
   to tests . . .

they're all here.

We tell you what to do when a manuscript has been accepted—
and what to do when it has been rejected—and we try to keep
your spirits up all the way through. Who else gives you a pat on
the back before you've even started?

We hope you enjoy reading this book as much as we have
enjoyed writing it. And we hope it helps you become . . .

A Productive Author!!!

CHAPTER ONE

How Do You Start?

So, you want to get published? "Certainly," you say, "doesn't everybody?" You may well be right. According to an old saying, there's at least one good book in the heart of every one of us! Remember those daydreams . . . If I just had the time to sit down and write all those great thoughts, I, too, would be on the best seller list . . . And when all that money comes rolling in from the royalties . . . "Where will it be, Dear, Acapulco this year or the Riveria?" Ah, yes, . . . dream on . . . The only problem is, first you have to write that best seller, and then you must find a publisher who agrees that you do, indeed, have a best seller and that it is worthy of publication.

If you are like most of us, you sometimes get confused between daydreams and reality, and you may need some help to separate them. Most authors have been there. The purpose of this book is to help you become productive, and the best way to begin is to answer the question, "How do you get started?"

First, just what do you have in mind to create?

A novel . . .
   A textbook . . .
      An article for a professional journal . . .

A book of poetry . . .
   A travel guide . . .
      A "How to do Something Book" . . .

A book of cross word puzzles . . .
   A children's book with or without illustrations . . .
      A cookbook . . .

A piece of original research . . .
  A biography or autobiography . . .
    An illustrated book of art . . .

A resource book . . .
  A short story . . .
    A new kind of test . . .
      A magazine article . . .

Whatever your category, you are faced with the problem of identifying a need for it, if you ever hope to see it in print. You must order your thinking. The initial fantasy of writing and publishing can be mind-boggling, but sooner or later you must face reality. The first question confronting you is, can you . . .

ESTABLISH THE NEED FOR YOUR PUBLICATION

Your reason for writing speaks somewhat to the need, so list the needs for your publication as you perceive them. You must be able to talk about this at the very beginning of your discussions with a publisher.

You should become knowledgeable of other publications on the market that might be considered competition.

Why is yours better? Do you have
  . . . more complete coverage?
    . . . a different approach?
      . . . a new innovation?

Is it
  . . . funnier?
    . . . sadder?
      . . . more complete?
        . . . more concise?
  . . . more optimistic?
    . . . more thought provoking?

Whatever you have to offer, can you demonstrate to a publisher why your proposal will better satisfy the market, and thus better meet the "need"?

If you can produce a good positive statement establishing the need for your publication, you may feel fairly confident that it will provoke the interest of a publisher—and that's half of the battle won right there!

Are you ready to start writing now?

No . . . not yet . . . for your next move is to . . .

IDENTIFY YOUR AUDIENCE OR MARKET

Who do you think will want to buy your book? use your game? or take your test? It is not uncommon for a publisher to ask these questions of an author. It may come as a surprise, but *you* actually are an expert in your field. Often a publisher really is seeking guidance and information from you, so be prepared with data on anticipated audiences and markets. Such information should include:

Age—what is the maturity level of the audience?

Educational level—how sophisticated should the language and material be?

Interests—how does your idea relate to identifiable interests of the audience?

Need—how will your publication help the reader to satisfy his needs?

Market—how can your publication be marketed most advantageously? Through regular bookstores? newsstands? specialty bookstores? college bookstores? ads in professional journals? sample copies to the field? direct sales to volume users?

Retail price range—what are the price expectations and ability to pay of your anticipated audience? Is it a hardback book audience or paperback?

Size of market—can you identify the size of the anticipated market? limited? unlimited? dependent upon sales approach? new field? a field past the point of high interest?

Some readers may feel that these items are the publisher's worries and that the author should not have to be concerned. Basically, this is the case—but the author that can recognize the limitations or expectations of the market will be more realistic in his anticipation of success.

Now? Now do you start writing?

No, . . . for the next step now is for you to . . .

STATE YOUR PURPOSE

A statement of purpose need not be elaborate or longwinded. It must, however, speak specifically and directly to the purpose of developing your material. For example, the statement of purpose for this particular book was as follows:

> To meet the tremendous demand from the thousands of writers who want a handbook telling them how to be successful in becoming published.

This was followed by a brief supporting paragraph:

> The success of previously being published has caused hundreds of inquiries to be directed at the authors—from professional associates, students, friends, even strangers. The essence of the questions—"You are published, how can *I* get published?" This has reached such proportions that one has to recognize that the market potential must be worthy of serious consideration.

Both of these statements came only after the authors had spent considerable time developing their ideas. An observer might conclude that it certainly should not have been very difficult to produce this statement—and it wasn't *after* we had discussed, debated, evaluated, synthesized, and written and rewritten to the purpose until we finally reduced it to its simplest and most direct form.

Once you have done the same thing, you will then, and only then, really begin to know that you have the substance of your creation under control. The statement of purpose will be referred to constantly throughout your writing—thus, it must be adequately stated.

If it develops that the purpose does not fully describe your intent, it will be necessary to restate it. If, however, you find that you have strayed or deviated from your stated purpose, then you are in error and must reorient your thinking within the confines of your statement.

Is it time to start writing yet? No, for once you have perfected your statement of purpose, you must . . .

DEVELOP THE TABLE OF CONTENTS

The task of developing a Table of Contents forces you to become organized. All of the topics and ideas contained in your writing must be placed in a logical sequence that will carry the reader from the introduction of your subject to the conclusion of your stated purpose. The most productive and successful method yet devised is explained below.

Obtain a supply (50 to 100) of 5 " x 7 " cards lined on one side. Start brainstorming by writing down one idea or one topic on each card. The secret to this process is that there is to be no rationalization . . . no justification as to the value or merit of any given idea. Just write it down as fast as the thoughts come to your mind, *one idea only to a card.*

Inspirations don't necessarily come in sequence or logical order, so don't be concerned that your thoughts seem to jump about in a grasshopper fashion. Right now, just be concerned with getting your thoughts on the cards. You will find that your mind will leap all over the subject. Some ideas may be great for chapter headings—others may show up as sub-sub headings. Some may not be worth the cards they are written on, but at this point, *just write them down.*

How long should this go on? A fair answer is "until you have covered your subject." This could be accomplished in a matter of hours for some authors, weeks for others. The amount of time involved is not important—the need to cover your subject is!

Once you are fairly confident that your cards represent the key thoughts and ideas or the characters, subplots, and plots of your project, you are ready to decide on the sequence of the cards and the establishment of the chapter or major headings.

Figure 1 shows how to approach this sequencing easily. If

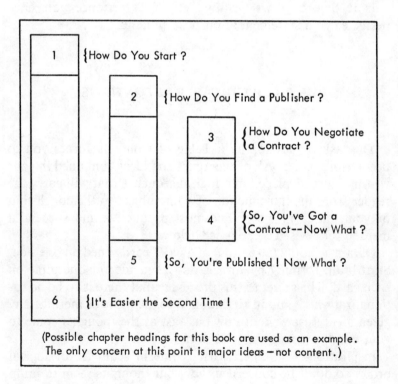

Figure 1
Organization of Ideas

you separate your cards according to the numbered blocks, your project will fall quickly into order.

Having sequenced your major areas, it is much easier to organize your chapter groupings. Again, use the technique of brainstorming. With a particular chapter in mind, write down only one idea on each card. When you are fairly confident that you have covered the topic, separate the ideas into logical order, and you will see each chapter begin to develop. Subheadings will emerge as you place each card in its relative position.

At this point, you begin to question the value of various ideas. Weigh the merits of one against the other or of one against your entire thesis. You may test your points or story lines on colleagues, friends, or family. Some ideas may be discarded; new ones will surface and be incorporated into the project.

The value of the card system becomes evident as you experience the ease with which your ideas can be transferred from one heading to another without disrupting the entire organization. Entire chapters can be moved about until you become satisfied with your final result. It is an ideal system for flexibility, and you will find it invaluable to your overall project.

Now is an excellent time for experimentation. Try the cards in different sequences, different approaches. Change the order of some of the old "tried and true" ideas of your specialty. Perhaps this is where you can become innovative and develop the "different" material that will cause your publication to become the most popular one in the field.

Once you are satisfied with the organization and sequence of your cards, type the major divisions as a tentative Contents page or story outline. It will be your guide for the rest of your project. You may alter it as you develop your writing, but you will find it impossible to function without it. It is the framework of the entire venture, and most prospective publishers will examine it with great care.

Now . . . are you ready to start writing? No, . . . there is yet another step. You first must . . .

ESTABLISH YOUR FORMAT

Before you begin to write, you should visualize the form, or format, or your finished publication.

What size should the printed page be . . .

What size and kind of typeface would be best . . .

Should it be a hardback or paperback . . .

Do you have anything to say about such things? Yes, with many publishers you do. There are limitations concerning costs of manufacture, quality of paper, and marketing (which your publisher will relate to you); however, if you see your proposal as having special format requirements to be properly presented, you must outline them in your recommendation to the publisher.

When you examined the competition publications, as we suggested earlier to "Establish the Need for Your Publication," you must have noticed their formats. How many pages did they contain? How many pages do you visualize in your finished product? Make copies of particular designs of material treatment that demonstrate what you have in mind.

Can you develop a unique page layout . . .

Can you develop a particularly expressive technique to convey your ideas through drawings or photographs? . . .

What kind of illustrations will be most effective? . . . cartoons? . . . photos? . . . artist illustrations? . . .

Will your narratives be highlighted with case studies? . . . or charts . . . or graphs? . . .

You should try to determine what best promotes and augments your material.

Some novelists have been successful through the use of lower case type only, that is, no capitals. Others have chosen to ignore most punctuation, paragraphs, and even chapters—but . . . be careful . . . this does not work for all novelists. It has worked for those who designed their material to be best reflected in that particular format.

What is best for you? Only you and your future publisher will be able to make that decision.

What about the use of color? Will it be a necessary part of some of the illustrations? Color adds a great deal of expense to the cost of manufacture and, consequently, to the retail price. A printing technique called *screening* can give a semblance of color within the color of ink used. Black ink can be screened to produce various shades of gray, or blue ink can be controlled to range from dark to light. This method often is used to good effect with little extra cost.

Charts and graphs may necessitate the use of color for more effectiveness. If color is anticipated, you must indicate this with your submission of copy to the prospective publisher.

What kind and size of type will accomplish your purpose most effectively? The type determines the number of characters per inch of finished copy. Once you decide upon a recommended page size, you can estimate the number of words per line and the number of lines per page and arrive at an estimate of the number of pages of copy in your finished work. A type chart showing style and size is shown in Figure 2.

Chapter headings and subheadings are often treated with distinctive type style and design. Have you considered this? If not, examine the books and publications at your local library or bookstore. You may find this to be a very profitable use of your time.

Once you have arrived at fairly definite recommendations for the format of your proposal, you are . . . finally . . . READY TO START WRITING! . . . for your next step is to . . .

Sizes of Type

This is a sample of 6 point type

This is a sample of 8 point type

This is a sample of 10 point type

This is a sample of 12 point type

This is a sample of 14 point type

Roman

Baskerville

Sans Serif

Futura Medium

Script

Thompson Quillscript

Black Letter

Goudy Text

Figure 2
Type Size and Style

DEVELOP AN APPROPRIATE SAMPLE

Your prospective publisher will want a sample of your writing to evaluate not only your writing skill but also the form and format you have suggested. Your ability is usually best demonstrated by the development of at least one chapter or section of the proposed work. This sample should be done in a complete and finished form. Some writers are capable of editing their own material; however, if you doubt your own editing ability, it might be wise to seek assistance from an associate, an editor, an English teacher, or even a professional writer.

A critique of your work at this point may be beneficial. One word of caution—if your proposal is new and different—possibly even radically so—from the accepted norms, you may find that you must have faith in your own judgment. It is not uncommon to experience negative critiques, which, rather than relating to your writing or expression, really reflect resistance to the ideas that you are suggesting.

Writing for publication is a very personal experience. You may be subjected to unsolicited advice and observations from friends and associates, but you are the final decision maker. It is your work, and you are going to enjoy the success or failure of it. Keep your objectives in mind at all times to avoid forces that might distract you from their fulfillment.

Once you have completed a satisfactory sample, you will be in a better position to estimate the overall size of your finished product. By referring to your tentative Contents page, you can estimate how the other sections or chapter will compare in length.

If you are dealing with a game, a poem, or other type of rather short material, simply submit the entire work. However, protect yourself with a common law copyright statement, such as the following:

> This material is the sole property of (your name). It is not to be sold, reproduced, or generally distributed without written consent.

Although not a legal copyright, it does identify you as the originator of the material should it become lost or misplaced, or fall into the hands of other than a professional publisher.

Should you plan to distribute (free or otherwise) any copy of any of your material, you should assure your common law copyright by placing a statement of ownership on the first page. Distribution in any form constitutes publication, and it places the material into the public domain if it is not properly protected.

If you prefer to hold the copyright of a complete product, such as a poem, the statutory fee for registration of a copyright claim is $4, payable to the Copyright Office, Library of Congress, Washington, D.C. 20059.

You are ready, at this point, to . . .

ORGANIZE A PUBLISHER'S PACKAGE

The most important part of a publisher's package is a letter that will capture the interest of the publisher to such an extent that consideration will be given to the material you have prepared. You should speak briefly and concisely to the following points:

1. Need
2. Audience or market
3. Purpose

It is also recommended that you speak to the enclosure of the following items:

1. Table of Contents
2. Sample format
3. Sample chapter

The sample letter in Figure 3 is a simulated letter written by the authors for this book. It is included to illustrate how these items can be spoken to briefly but inclusively.

```
The Unique Publishing Company
1000 Park Place
Empire City, New York                          December 10, 1976


                    SUBJECT:  Publication Proposal

                    "CAREER EDUCATION GUIDANCE KIT"

Gentlemen:

The major problem confronting our nation's educators today is how to
include "Career Education" in an already overloaded school curriculum.

The U. S. Office of Education has mandated that all fifty state depart-
ments of education effectively incorporate the concept of career
education throughout our entire educational structure, K-16 and into
continuing education for a life-time experience.

The typical classroom teacher has had little, if any, experience in the
world of business or industry.  Nevertheless, in addition to all other
responsibilities, he is now expected to be a source of knowledge and
expertise regarding "Career Education."

Having worked in the field of vocational and career education for more
than 20 years, I feel qualified to address this problem.  I have de-
veloped a "Career Education Guidance Kit," which is written to the three
levels:  Elementary; Junior High; and High School/Junior College.

You can readily see the market potential of this publication.  Every
teacher, student, counselor, or librarian who has access to the "Kit"
can instantly be an informed person on some 700 occupations described
under the headings of the 15 USOE Occupational Clusters.

Enclosed is a sample of the kit, demonstrating the design and treatment
of the material in the occupational cluster, CONSTRUCTION.  I have
selected your publishing firm because of its reputation and coverage in
the field of elementary and secondary education.

Please inform me of your interest in this publication at your earliest
convenience as I do not plan to solicit other publishers until I hear
from you.

                              Sincerely,




                              A. N. Author
                              3078 La Canada Drive
                              Jacksonville, Florida 32216


Enclosure:  Sample of Kit Material
```

Figure 3
Sample Letter to Publisher

Now that you have gone this far, you will be interested in
reading Chapter 2 . . .

CHAPTER TWO

How Do You Find A Publisher?

Finding a publisher has been a stumbling block to untold numbers of aspiring writers. The fear of the unknown is really worse than the reality of doing.

Some writers (perhaps unaware of their own professional standing) fear that their material is not suitable for acceptance, so they don't even try to find a publisher. Others just fear rejection. Still others find it beyond belief that they have produced something that is marketable, that they are equal to other authors who have appeared in print; that *their* names can appear on the cover of a book—so the manuscript remains hidden in a drawer!

Yet, the daydreams persist. "Someday I'll be published." "Someday I'll be famous and make a lot of money! Well, look at Grace Metalious and her book, Peyton Place!"

Yes, look at Grace Metalious!—and the thousands of other successful authors. Success came *only* after they had made an effort to find a publisher. Their manuscripts were not hidden in a drawer, they did not lack confidence in their own ability.

It is time . . . now . . . to . . .

FIND OUT WHO PUBLISHES IN YOUR AREA

Have you become familiar with the publications on the market—your "competition"—as you were directed to do in Chapter One when you established the need for your publication? If so, you have the names and addresses of the publishers. Each of them now represents a possible publisher for *your* material.

"Oh," you might say, "if a publisher already has a publication in this area, why would a similar proposal be considered?" Many large publishing houses have subsidiaries, and it is not uncommon for them to publish competitive materials. Publishers know that it takes a several products to sell to all of the potential customers in a given field. So, send in your publisher's package, and let the publisher decide what is wanted or not wanted. *Don't trap yourself by making the decision for them!*

There are numerous other sources for names and addresses of publishers in your field, one is at the back of this book in Appendix C. It is impossible here to cover all of the publishers in every field. If you need to investigate further, visit your local library. Don't waste your time groping about a library trying to find this information—ask the librarian. Librarians are expert researchers and are usually happy to assist you.

Retail bookstores are another source of potential publishers. If your field of publication is at the college level, inquire at a college bookstore. Most bookstore managers are sympathetic to this kind of request—just avoid the busy time of day. If your proposal is a specialty—, a game, test, "how to," or whatever—you may encounter some difficulty in locating a dealer; however, persistence pays off. Keep searching until you have the names and addresses of several potential publishers.

Many publishers have a large force of field representatives who call on retail bookstores, college professors, school teachers, and school book depositories. In addition to selling and servicing accounts in the field, these representatives are on the alert to locate authors who are developing materials for publication. It is their hope to find you and guide you to their publishing house. Someone may be looking for you just as hard as you are looking for them!

How can you locate a field representative? As you make your contacts seeking the names and addresses of publishers, ask for the name and addresses of field representatives at the same time. A brief letter of inquiry directed to a publisher usually will result in a reply informing you if a representative is available in your area. A quicker way of finding out is to make a phone call to a publisher (more on this subject later).

Your task is to . . .

PICK THE RIGHT PUBLISHER FOR YOU

Soliciting more than one publisher at a time is not fair—or ethical. You expect the publisher to give your work serious consideration, and this requires considerable time and effort by an editor. If your project appears to have promise, other departments may be called in. . . .

Manufacturing may be asked to estimate production costs . . .
Packaging might have to be considered . . .
Sales, Marketing, and Promotion will be consulted for estimates for marketing your publication . . .

Therefore, it is reasonable for the publisher to expect you to offer his firm the right to accept or reject your proposal without competition.

One of the authors of this book unwittingly violated every rule in finding a publisher when he first entered the ranks as an author. Drawing upon past experience as a salesman, he decided that, since he did not know one publisher from another, the logical thing to do was to solicit a whole group of them at one time. He selected 25, and sent a publisher's package to each one, all in one mailing! The results were somewhat amazing. Within three weeks, nine publishers had responded. Three were interested—one saved the day by sending an editor down to sign a contract quickly. Had the other two publishers been equally interested, a real problem of trying to deal fairly and equitably with them could have developed. In this case, luck was with the beginner, but now he knows better—just one publisher at a time!

How do you decide the best publisher for you? After you discover the most popular publishers in your field, as discussed in Chapter 1, narrow your choice further by considering how your proposal might "fit" among the other publications of a given publishing house. For instance, if you plan your work as an inexpensive paperback as opposed to an expensive hardback, obviously you should select the publisher that deals in paperbacks.

The size of a firm, or a "big" name, does not necessarily guarantee "big" results. What is important is to select a publisher who is known in your field, one who has a sales force that reaches the population for which your product is designed. If your proposal is for a textbook in high school science, be sure that your prospective publisher has a nationwide sales force calling on the secondary school trade to assure the market exposure it deserves. However, if your writing is oriented to a specific region, and the public interest is limited to that area, it is reasonable to assume that you might have more success with a publisher who markets only in that region.

There is no fixed set of rules to guide you. At best, we hope to introduce the variables that must be considered. The final decision is yours. If it seems that your first contact is less than what you had hoped for, remember that you make the decision of accepting or rejecting an offer.

Now that you have selected a publisher . . .

MAKE CONTACT WITH THE PUBLISHER OF YOUR CHOICE

Send a simple, direct letter to the publisher. Three or four short paragraphs are sufficient.

First paragraph—*explain why your publication fulfills a need.*
Second paragraph—*identify your audience or market.*

Third paragraph—*state your purpose.*

A closing statement should explain that you have a *publisher's package* containing a *Table of Contents,* a *suggested format,* and a *sample chapter* ready to forward by return mail.

Simple? Yes, partly because at this point you have everything you need to write such a letter. Remember: Keep it simple, to the point, and *only one page long!*

If you want to address your letter to an editor, pick up the telephone and call the chosen publishing house. Tell the switchboard operator that you want to be connected to the editor in charge of publications related to your proposal. When connected, identify yourself and ask for the name of the editor. If you have been connected with the correct office, the secretary will usually give you the first information you need—name of the editor. He may also know whether the publishing house is interested in new manuscripts in your area, how extensive the sales and distribution of the product are, and if the editor would be interested in receiving your publisher's package.

If you are fortunate enough to talk with the editor, you will find that he is interested in what you have to say—and he may very well be interested in seeing your publisher's package. Of course you may be told that he is not interested, for a variety of reasons. If that happens, ask for suggestions of a publisher who might be interested. Sometimes you get excellent leads this way.

Whatever the response, the two or three dollars spent on a telephone call is money well spent. Think of it as a psychological breakthrough—you talked to a publishing house! maybe even an editor! At least you now know the name of the editor who should receive your publisher's package . . . so-o-o . . . mail it! . .

and anxiously await for . . .

THE PUBLISHER'S RESPONSE

Publishers may respond within two to four weeks after receiving a proposal from an author. (Some take a good deal longer.) Since this is a period of extreme anguish for the new author, be sure to send your proposal by certified mail. You are thus assured that your work was received, and you also have legal evidence that you submitted your package to the publisher.

There are three possible responses that you can expect:

1. *Acceptance* will come in the form of a letter from an editor. If your publisher's package was complete, concise, and well presented, the response may be brief but to the point. They like your proposal, they are interested in entering into a contract with you, the contract will be forthcoming shortly, and they are looking forward to working with you on what should be a most successful project.

2. *Acceptance with reservations* will speak to the overall acceptancy by the publisher, but there are one or more points or items they wish to consider before fully committing to a contract. You will be told exactly what the concerns are and you will be asked to respond to them.

3. *Rejection.* No message is more disheartening to an author than the letter from the publisher saying that his proposal was interesting— but! Later we will go into greater detail as to what you should do if and/or when you receive this response. For now, let it be pointed out that few authors are inexperienced in receiving rejections. It really is part of your development. Writing is one of the most demanding skills, and success usually comes only after much hard work and numerous attempts.

Figures 4, 5, and 6 show sample letters exchanged between a fictitious publisher and the authors of an imaginary work. Encouraged by the positive response, the authors immediately went to work on the additional sample requested in Figure 4, and submitted it on January 30, 1977 (see Fig. 5). On February 15, 1977 the letter shown in Figure 6, indicating acceptance and enclosure of contracts, was sent by the publisher. The contract was signed by both authors and returned. It was then signed by the publisher, and on February 22 the agreement was completed. The total amount of time involved was approximately three months.

If you have followed the suggestions in Chapter 2 to this point, you know who publishes in your area of interest, you have picked a publisher, you have made contact by letter or

⇉UNIQUE⇇
PUBLISHING COMPANY

1000 PARK PLACE

January 20, 1977

Mr. A. N. Author
3078 La Canada Drive
Jacksonville, Florida 32216

Dear Mr. Author:

Thank you for writing us regarding your "Career
Education Guidance Kit."

Career education appears to be a very timely subject in the education field and your proposal
seems to fit the qualifications for publication.
To be salable to schools, it would be advisable
to have the cluster categories correspond with the
U. S. Office of Education recommendations as well
as with the specifics at each of the grade levels.

Please submit to us one more sample occupational
cluster so that we may be assured that the above
points are adequately covered. If this second
sample looks as good as the first, we should be
in the position to offer an immediate agreement
to publish.

Sincerely,

EMPIRE CITY, N.Y.

B. K. Editor

Figure 4
Acceptance—with Reservation

Mr. B. K. Editor   January 30, 1977
The Unique Publishing Company
1000 Park Place
Empire City, New York

Dear Mr. Editor:

Your prompt response to the proposal for the "Career Education Guidance Kit" is most appreciated and encouraging.

Enclosed, as you requested, is an additional sample of another occupational cluster. I feel confident that you will find that all of the major points as specified by the USOE recommendations have been more than adequately covered. To reassure you on this point, I have enclosed some USOE literature concerning career education that will verify my statement.

I am hoping that this sample will fulfill your expectations and that I will receive an early reply with an agreement for contract enclosed.

                          Sincerely,

                          A. N. Author
                          3078 La Canada Drive
                          Jacksonville, Florida 32216

Enclosures: Sample
             USOE literature

Figure 5

Response to Acceptance with Reservation Letter

⇉UNIQUE⇇
PUBLISHING COMPANY

1000 PARK PLACE

February 15, 1977

Mr. A. N. Author
3078 La Canada Drive
Jacksonville, Florida 32216

Dear Mr. Author:

It is our pleasure to enclose two copies of our
Unique Publishing Company contracts. Please examine
the contract carefully, then sign, initial each page
and return both copies to this office. You will be
sent your copy when it has been signed by an official
of our firm.

You will be hearing from the production editor
assigned to your project shortly. We are looking
forward to working with you. Please contact me if
you have any questions in the meantime. We feel
that this should become a very successful publication.

Sincerely,

EMPIRE CITY, N.Y.

B. K. Editor

Enclosures: 2

Figure 6
Acceptance Letter

phone, and you know the three possible responses awaiting you. You are ready now to make the major move—submit your publisher's package.

We hope you don't have to be concerned with . . .

WHAT DO YOU DO WHEN YOU HAVE BEEN REJECTED?

A rejection—or perhaps you would prefer to call it a "nonacceptance"—is never a happy piece of news (see Figure 7). However, it can prove valuable. Work not accepted for publication indicates the need for some serious analysis. Once the initial shock and disappointment have subsided (it seldom ever goes away) you must confront yourself with an evaluation.

Viewing the reasons given by the publisher (most publishers give some explanation for a rejection) as to why they cannot publish your proposal, refer to the key points of your publisher's package as outlined in Chapter 1.

1. *Statement of need*—could you have been more specific in your explanation of why the market needs your publication?
2. *Audience or market*—did you overlook some major areas of your perceived market? Could you have produced more solid figures or data?
3. *Statement of purpose*—was it as logical, forceful, or compelling as it might have been?
4. *Table of Contents*—was this too brief? Too involved? Did it really speak to the content as intended?
5. *Format*—could it have been more distinctive? How could the format better display the content?
6. *Sample chapter*—is the writing style on a professional level comparable to other publications? Did you select the best chapters to demonstrate your writing, layout, and format?

If you find that you can make some positive revisions in your publisher's package, this should be your first effort. Remember that your presentation in this package must be as nearly perfect as you feel capable of producing—it is your sales tool, and your only opportunity to sell your idea.

THE P_J EDUCATION
PUBLISHERS

LAKEFRONT DRIVE   —   MOTORTOWN, MICH.

Mr. A. N. Author
3078 La Canada Drive   September 15, 1976
Jacksonville, Florida 32216

Dear Mr. Author:

Thank you for your letter of July 30 and the proposal for the "Career Education Guidance Kit." Your phone call relative to the project was very informative.

The samples you forwarded were most complete and comprehensive. Your proposal is sound and does very definitely fill a pressing need among curricula materials.

It is with sincere regret that I have to tell you that because of our previous commitments and a cutback in our development budget we will not be able to consider your proposal for publication at this time.

This is in no way a reflection on the quality of your material or publishing concept. I would recommend that you explore this proposal with another publisher. Should there be a change in our plans regarding a new item in our line perhaps we can once again reconsider this project.

                                        Sincerely,

                                        Patricia Jamison, Editor
                                        College Division

NMN

Figure 7
Non-Acceptance Letter

Once you are satisfied that your proposal is as complete as you can make it, review the list of potential publishers from your initial approach and select the one that you feel will be your next best prospect. Go through the contact process (by phone or correspondence) and send off the publisher's package again. Use certified mail again, too. How many times should you do this? As many times as you have publishers' names and the persistence to keep trying.

Author Leon Uris (*Trinity, OB VII, Topaz, Exodus*) is reported to have worked for two years on his first novel, *Battle Cry,* only to be turned down by a dozen publishers before finding one that would accept the book in 1953. Hailed by reviewers, it became an enduring best seller.

Rosemary Rogers (*Sweet Savage Love, Dark Fires*), a divorcee with four children who researched her books during lunch hours on her office job and wrote in the evenings, received acceptance notices on her unsolicited manuscripts four weeks after sending each in. Both titles became best sellers.

If you are convinced that your publication fills a need, has a market, and is on a par with other professional writings of its kind, keep looking for a publisher.

It's possible that you might end up asking . . .

WHY NOT PUBLISH YOUR OWN WORK?

The frustrations involved with trying to find a publisher often lead a writer to thoughts of publishing his own work. This is not an impossibility. A number of authors have done it successfully. However, there are many problems confronting the self-published author.

1. Money. It takes considerable capital to finance a publication. The only way that the unit cost of a printed piece can be significantly reduced is through large volume printing. Seldom

is an individual capable of financing a first printing sizable enough to keep the costs down to the point where the retail sales price is not prohibitive. Remember that your competition in the marketplace has employed every cost-reducing opportunity to be able to sell at a competitive price, and large volume is only one of the cost-reducing steps involved.

2. Sales. The name of the publishing business is sales. It does no good to have a large volume first printing unless you also have the ability to distribute and sell your product. National and regional publishers have sales staffs that know the industry and call on the trade in every major market in the country. The competition is fierce. It is an extraordinary individual author who can mount a sales campaign that will produce an adequate return on invested time and money.

3. Professional talents. The individual author must possess the talent and knowledge to write at a professional level, but he also must be able to design format and layouts, edit, proofread, specify type, direct the art work, take photographs, draw charts, negotiate with printing houses, effect the sales and distribution of the finished product—and the list goes on and on.

Prospective authors can see their work in print by responding to advertisements in newspapers and magazines. These ads often bear headlines such as "Authors Wanted" or "We Want People Who Can Write." The message says that a certain publisher is seeking manuscripts . . . just write to them or visit their representative when he comes to town. Often the implication is that you can get published through their service or, perhaps, you just need to take an author's aptitude test. Some people may get published this way, but it should be pointed out that sometimes a fee is required or a program to help improve writing style is involved, with no guarantee of publication upon completion of the program.

Most authors have found it beneficial to deal directly with known publishers in their fields. If your work has quality and if the market is identifiable, there usually will be a publisher who will recognize this—and pay for your time and efforts.

Now you are ready to learn .

CHAPTER THREE

How Do You Negotiate A Contract?

Authors tend to talk about contracts . . . but . . .

AGREEMENT IS THE NAME OF THE GAME

A "contractual agreement" is the popular terminology for making a contract with a publisher. The connotation is that a considerable exchange goes on between an author and the editor regarding the treatment of material, emphasis of subject matter, and marketability of the total product. The prime object of all parties concerned is to produce the most successful publication. The author should keep in mind that "agreement" is a two-way street, and not be overwhelmed by the experience of dealing with an editor. Remember, your views and opinions are the expression of an expert in your field, just as the editor is an expert in his field, so there are agreements to be made by both parties.

The author should understand a few basics of the publishing business before entering into agreement discussions.

WHAT IS A CONTRACTUAL AGREEMENT?

Simply described, a contractual agreement states that you, the author, agree to write according to the specifications of the sample you submit. The publisher agrees to publish and market the material, provided your subsequent work maintains the professional quality and style demonstrated, and to pay you a royalty on all copies sold.

Disagreement—What Do You Do About It?

The publisher may suggest additions or deletions to the manuscript. This may occur before, during, or after the signing of the contractual agreement. The author may or may not agree to some of the suggestions. If the editor's observations are valid and you see how your work would be enhanced by including the suggestions, it is in order for the author to follow such recommendations. However, should you find the suggestions in violation of some of your basic concepts, you must defend your position. If a difference of opinion develops into a basic point of disagreement between you and the editor, it must be resolved to the satisfaction of both parties. Otherwise, you face an impasse that could prompt you or the publisher to withdraw from the contractual agreement.

An extreme degree of misunderstanding between author and editor usually can be avoided if you know certain things before you sign the agreement.

WHAT WILL BE EXPECTED OF THE AUTHOR?

The author actually establishes the expectations for his performance when organizing the publisher's package (see Chapter 1). It is there that you outline your perception of the treatment of the material and its content. Your sample demonstrates your ability to write to the subject. If there are any major differences to be discussed, usually it is done in the early stages, and compromises are made prior to entering into the contractual agreement.

Working With An Editor

Somewhere in the early stages of negotiations, the publisher will assign an editor to your project. It will be the editor's responsibility to assist, counsel, guide, and encourage you. The role of an editor is of particular value to an author. Proof of this is found in the acknowledgments of authors who have expressed their gratitude to their editors for help and guidance throughout the trying times of literary creation. If a broad statement might be made about the editorial staffs of publishing houses, one can say that they are generally tactful, knowledgeable in their fields, gracious to their authors, and it is a genuine pleasure to work with them. So, once you have been introduced to your editor, you may feel secure in the knowledge that all efforts involved will be directed toward making your work a success and you a successful author.

Production and marketing departments of the larger publishing houses may have need for direct contact with you. Therefore, additional editors may be assigned to work with you on specific aspects of your project as it progresses toward completion.

Establishing A Time Schedule

A publisher is faced with the very real problem of time. He must schedule the writing of the original manuscript, its editing, printing, manufacture, advertising, promotion, sales, and distribution. For the project to move smoothly toward the target date for publication, the author must commit to a fairly fixed schedule. Steps in manuscript publication from the author's viewpoint are shown in Figure 8. A schedule for completion of these steps is a negotiable point, and you should have a realistic idea of your ability to produce the material within a given time period. You must take into consideration all of your

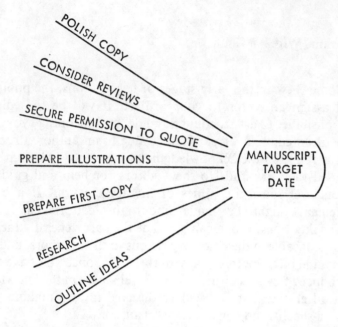

Figure 8

Steps to Manuscript Publication (Author's Viewpoint)

other responsibilities—family, friends, job, recreation, and other personal concerns.

Avoid undue pressure by allowing yourself time to meet your contractual agreements within your life-style. Your publisher may request a submission of chapters, sections, or units on specific dates, or you may agree on just one date for submission of the total work. Whatever, set a schedule in which you can produce the finished product with the professional quality of your original sample and still maintain some semblance of a normal life.

Reviews of Your Manuscript

Some publishers have a standard procedure of sending new manuscript copy to "readers" or "reviewers" for critiques and evaluation. Reviewers are professionals in the subject field of the work, and they serve as consultants to the publisher. Critiques from reviewer may be sent to you for consideration. You will be expected to receive them in the professional manner in which they are given, for the purpose is to improve the manuscript. (Reviews are discussed in greater detail in Chapter 4.)

Securing Permission to Use Quoted Material

The author usually is expected to secure all permissions for the use of any quoted or reproduced copyrighted material. This is the author's responsibility, and permissions should be obtained *before* the manuscript is sent to the publisher . . . and *should be in written form.*

Address your request to the publisher of the journal or book from which the material is taken, cite the quote you wish to use, and explain why you wish to use it. Figure 9 shows an example of such a request letter.

When you have received permission to use the quotation, make a copy of the letter and forward the original with your manuscript. Keep the copy with your notes.

Some publishers or authors may require a fee for the privilege of reprinting a quotation. The payment of this fee may be the responsibility of the author. Proof of payment must be made available to the publisher. Some publishers will pay the fee, others will pay and then deduct it from your royalties.

Providing Drawings and Illustrations

Many authors assume that the drawings and illustrations indicated in their original manuscript are automatically the responsibility of the publisher. This is not necessarily the case. The publisher may ask the author if the art, drawings, photographs, or illustrations are to be furnished by the author or the publisher. The reason for the inquiry is to establish the

July 27, 1976

TO: Copyright & Permissions Editor
      Prentice-Hall, Inc.
      Englewood Cliffs, N. J. 07632

FROM: Dr. Philip J. Gearing
      7830 Las Canas Ct.
      Jacksonville, Fla. 32216

Gentlemen:

I am preparing a book on __HOW TO GET PUBLISHED__ to be published by Prentice-Hall, Inc. May I please have your permission to include the following material from Prentice-Hall Author's Guide:

A sample permission letter, page 15

in my book and in future revisions and editions thereof, including non-exclusive world rights in all languages. These rights will in no way restrict republication of your material in any other form by you or others authorized by you. Should you not control these rights in their entirety, would you kindly let me know whom else I must write.

Unless you indicate otherwise, I will use the following credit line:

Prentice-Hall's Author Guide;
New Jersey; Prentice-Hall, Inc.
1962

I would greatly appreciate your consent to this request. For your convenience a release form is provided below and a copy of this letter is enclosed for your files.

Very sincerely yours,

Philip J. Gearing

_____

I (We) grant permission for the use requested above.

                    _____

                    _____

            Date_____

Figure 9

Sample Permission Form. Reprinted by permission of Prentice-Hall, Inc.

responsibility for paying the cost of these expensive items, which can have a bearing on the size of the royalty the publisher offers the writer.

If you can supply the necessary illustrations, the publisher will have less costs involved and the author may be able to secure a better share of the royalties. This point will be discussed during your negotiations, so consider it prior to any agreement talks.

Reading Galley Proofs

Galley proofs are the first printed copy you will see of your finished manuscript. You will be expected to read the proofs carefully, correcting all errors, and return them to the publisher. Chapter 4 shows the editing marks to use and discusses galley proof editing in greater depth.

Cooperating With Other Departments

You will be expected to cooperate with any of the departments of the publishing firm if they request information from you. Marketing, for example, may ask that you submit lists of potential users of your book—people who might be helpful in promoting sales; names of newspapers or publications in which ads might reach the specific market for your publication.

You are more familiar with those who are interested in your book than the publisher's staff can possibly be. It is to your benefit to cooperate with these requests and furnish all information possible. (See Fig. 10-Author's Information)

Second Edition Revisions

When your publication has been on the market for a time and a new edition is being considered by your publisher, you will be asked to suggest any minor revisions. If major changes are

```
(TO FOLLOW:  COOPERATING WITH OTHER DEPARTMENT)

An author should be ready to respond to the following queries:

                           AUTHOR'S INFORMATION


Summary of Book            Summarize in a short paragraph (50-75 words)
                           the purpose, thrust, and intent of the book.

Significant Features
of the Book                Describe briefly four or five main points to
                           be found in the book.  Highlight outstanding
                           findings or features, including illustrations.

Competition in the
Field                      Identify the unique attributes of the book that
                           will highlight the successful competition with
                           other publications on the market.

Course Possibilities
of This Book               Identify the courses in which you feel the book
                           could be used as a text.  Specify the school
                           level or college year.  Describe any other
                           market possibilities.

Biographical
Information                List any other publications you have written.
                           Identify any awards or recognitions that would
                           help establish you as an authority in your
                           field.  Include any promotional material that
                           would be beneficial in marketing the book.
```

Figure 10
Author's Information

needed, it will be your responsibility to update your book and perhaps rewrite entire portions. You may need to update illustrations, photographs, dates, and other data. This will be your opportunity to revitalize your publication.

Now that you have a better idea of what is expected of the author . . . you also need to know . . .

WHAT WILL BE EXPECTED OF THE PUBLISHER?

The publisher assigns editors to work with authors. The editor is responsible for obtaining reviews of the author's work to assure professional quality and need for publication prior to commiting the publisher to an agreement. Communication is maintained with the author, and assistance is extended when needed.

The publisher will set up the production schedule when the manuscript is nearing completion and may assign a production editor at the appropriate time. It is the production editor's responsibility to bring the completed publication off the press as near to schedule as possible.

Securing the Copyright

The publisher is usually responsible for taking out the copyright on the finished product. This protects both the author and the publisher. The copyright is usually but not always the in name of the publisher. It was for this reason that you were cautioned (in Chapter 1) to get the permission of the publisher before distributing any portions of your manuscript, whether you charged for the material or not. Once you are under contract, the material you produce is rightfully the publisher's as well as yours. You share an interest in it, and the interests must be mutually honored and guarded.

Under the new copyright law, you and the publisher are protected for a period of 50 years after the death of the author. So, all you have to do is write a best seller!

Marketing the Publication

It is the publisher's responsibility to bring the finished publication to market. Steps to publication from the publisher's viewpoint are shown in Figure 11. Among other

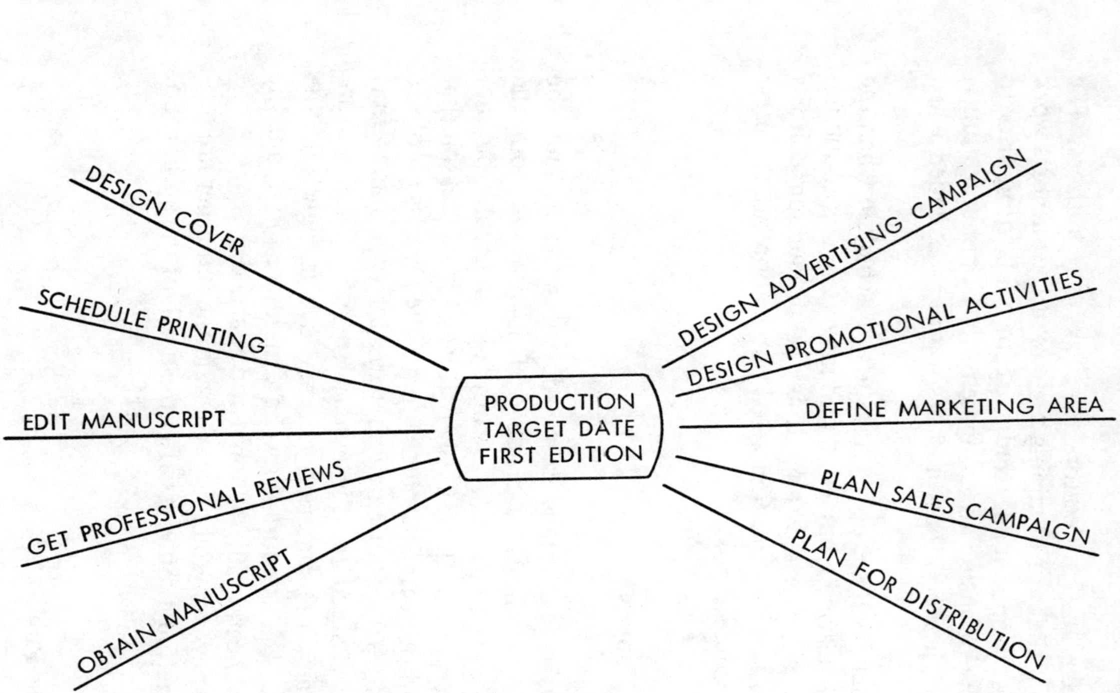
DESIGN COVER
SCHEDULE PRINTING
EDIT MANUSCRIPT
GET PROFESSIONAL REVIEWS
OBTAIN MANUSCRIPT
PRODUCTION
TARGET DATE
FIRST EDITION
DESIGN ADVERTISING CAMPAIGN
DESIGN PROMOTIONAL ACTIVITIES
DEFINE MARKETING AREA
PLAN SALES CAMPAIGN
PLAN FOR DISTRIBUTION

Figure 11

Steps to Manuscript Publication (Publisher's Viewpoint)

duties, the publisher supervises the selection of the book jacket or cover design; advertises in the appropriate media—journals, direct mail, trade papers, magazines; and employs a sales staff to promote and sell the new product. Often a sizable budget is assigned for the distribution of free samples to key potential users. One of the greatest sales forces is the testimonials by satisfied initial users; this is why your list of prospective buyers is so important. A good introduction of a book to the market is very critical to its ultimate success.

Free Copies For the Author! How Many?

First-time published authors usually are surprised (and sometimes disappointed) by the relatively small number of free copies made available to them. You may receive as few as three or as many as ten—but seldom more than that! The reason for the small number of copies is that books are expensive, and the publisher is not in the position to give you enough copies to hand out to your family and friends. So, you will just have to dig down into your own royalties and buy all those copies wholesale from the publisher. If you planned to make your book a gift to aunts, uncles, in-laws, friends, professional associates, and others, why don't you instead consider talking them into *buying* your book? You can autograph the copies, and the increased sales will help your royalties!

ROYALTIES! HOW MUCH?

Royalties paid by publishers vary according to a number of factors:

1. Will your book be marketed widely, perhaps internationally?
2. Is the market a rather limited one, such as a specialty area at a university level?

3. How high are the costs?
4. Is the author well known or unknown?

Publishing companies usually have previous experience on all of these factors, and they base their royalties on their statistics. How will you know if they are being fair? Well, basically you won't; you take them on faith, more or less. You can check with other authors, which will give you some idea of the market, but each book is different—costs are different, book markets are different, and there may be some variation even within the same publishing company.

Industry wide figures show, however, that the following royalty figures are fairly representative:

Paperback publications—6 to 12 percent
Hardback publications—10 to 18 per cent

Unknown authors can expect to be offered the lower end of the scale—proven authors are given the higher. Most publishers initially will state the royalty they are willing to offer at the outset of negotiations for the contractual agreement.

Negotiating for Royalties

The author has the option of accepting a publisher's royalty offer or countering with a figure he feels more nearly represents the value of the work. The publisher has the right to accept, reject, or counter with another offer. The author then is faced with the decision to accept or reject and attempt further negotiation.

A rejection on the author's part fosters the possibility of a stalemate, and he may be faced with finding a new publisher. However, the pressure on the unpublished author is usually so great that his desire to be published tends to reduce any aggressive negotiations.

The previously published author usually knows from experience whether he is being offered the "going rate" for royalty. If he feels a higher per cent is in order, he must be able to justify it on the basis of anticipated greater sales because of his name in the field, the content of the publication, or the better treatment of the subject. Some authors have been able to negotiate a royalty based on volume of sales. The rationale for this is that once the publisher recovers initial costs, there are more profits to be shared with the author. Such an agreement might read:

> 10% royalty on the sale of the first 10, 20, or 30,000 copies, and 15% on all sales thereafter.

The potential sales of a publication are the only real leverage that an author possesses—and seldom is he really aware or knowledgeable of the extent of this negotiating power.

Many authors use the services of literary agents to guide them through this whole negotiating process. Literary agents and their services are discussed in greater detail at the end of this chapter.

Whatever you do, try to conduct your negotiations in a friendly and constructive fashion. You don't want to lose the relationship that is so necessary to the success of your publication.

What Are Royalties Based On?

Usually royalties are based on the actual cash revenue received by the publisher, that is, the wholesale price of the publication. For example, if a hardback book retails for $15, and the publisher's wholesale price to the retailer is $10, a 15 per cent royalty to the author would amount to $1.50 per copy.

However, one must remember that publishers sell at different prices to different buyers, depending on the volume purchased. Books clubs, state departments of education, and book depositories are examples of large-volume buyers who purchase on individually negotiated prices. Consequently, the royalty earned by the author in this example is not a fixed dollar figure per book, but rather a fixed percentage of the publisher's actual cash revenue.

Some publishers pay a royalty based on the "list," or published retail, price of the book. Under this agreement, the per cent is usually considerably smaller than that paid on cash revenue to the publisher. As an example, let's take that same book that retails for $15. A royalty to the author based on list price would possibly be only 10 per cent, thus producing the same amount, $1.50, as the 15 per cent royalty based on cash revenue.

The publisher usually will have a fixed method by which the company operates, and it is pretty much up to the author to accept it.

Royalties—What Part of Gross Profit?

Sometimes concern is expressed that the author's percentage of royalty is too low when compared to the revenue percentage assigned to the publisher. But the publisher's figures do not represent the gross profit on the publication.

The publishing firm must pay all costs of the writing, editing, producing, advertising, distribution, and selling of the product. When the author's royalty is figured against the gross profit accrued to the publisher after all costs are paid, it comes more nearly to being anywhere from 25 to 40 per cent of the gross profit.

Since few authors can begin to muster the financial resources, publishing expertise, and salesmanship offered by a publisher, the large majority of authors elect to be published by reputable publishers on a royalty basis rather than embarking on a "do-it-yourself" publication.

Variables Affecting Royalties

The market potential of a publication has a great bearing on the author's royalty percentage. If a publication is expected to have a wide mass market appeal, the sales price probably will be adjusted to the lower side to encourage a higher volume of sales. Thus both the publisher and the author will tend to agree to a smaller percentage of profit on the anticipation of more dollars to be realized from greater sales. If a publication is anticipated to have a limited market, the price will likely be set on the higher side, resulting in a greater dollar profit per unit of sales. The author in this case might expect a higher royalty to make up for the lesser volume of unit sales.

The costs involved in the production of a publication affect its sales price—thus its marketability, and, therefore, the royalty returns to the author. Extensive use of expensive color processes, artwork, illustrations, high grade paper, and quality of binding all contribute to a higher selling price for the finished product. The common objective of the author and publisher is to produce a publication that has optimum sales potential in relation to quality, content, and price. Successful publishing is a very demanding and competitive business—it might qualify as an art form as well!

Inflation increases royalties   as the costs of publishing force up the selling price of your publication. The publisher has to keep up with the increasing costs of doing business. Since the author's royalty is based upon a percentage of the sales price, any increases will be reflected in additional dollars in your royalty check.

Estimating Royalties

A fortune teller with a crystal ball is needed when you try to estimate how much money you can expect to make from a publication. Few publishers will even hazard a guess on expected author income because of the multitude of variables that can affect success.

However, there are some indicators that might help to guide you toward a conservative estimate. The fact that the publisher signed you to a contractual agreement to publish is strong proof that your publication should sell enough copies to at least break even on the first printing. How many copies would this be? For a rough guide, refer to Table 1 below.

Table 1

First Printing Break-even Point for Various Types of Books

	Copies
Hardback books for general market, library and general sales	10,000
Limited editions—color, high quality, expensive	5,000
Paperback books—broad market—priced in the market	20,000–50,000
Publications that will easily sell annually	50,000–100,000
Best sellers—book club selections, state-adopted books	100,000–+

How much money does this mean to the author? It's a case of simple arithmetic as shown in the following example:

$$\frac{\text{Units sold}}{10,000} \quad \times \quad \frac{\text{Unit price}}{\$5} \quad \times \quad \frac{\text{Author's royalty}}{10\%}$$

$$10,000 \times \$5 = \$50,000 \text{ Dollar Sales}$$
$$\$50,000 \times 10\% = \$5,000 \text{ Author's Royalty}$$

The life of a publication must be considered when estimating its potential revenue. Best sellers often enjoy a quick surge in sales, but they tend to fade rather quickly. A select few do enjoy a continuing demand. Textbooks and "how-to" books are usually more slowly accepted, but once they make an impression in the market, they are apt to enjoy more sustained sales, perhaps even for a period of years. Each publication has a marketability of its own. Only time in the marketplace will prove its success.

Accounting and Payment of Royalties

Most publishers make a semiannual accounting and payment of royalties to their authors; however, this is not a fixed or mandatory practice. Some publishers prefer to settle only once a year (not usually preferred by authors). This point should be established in discussions on the contractual agreement. Most authors want to know every six months how many copies of their publication have sold and to receive a check for the previous six months accounting period. You may meet a publisher who does not want to divulge the number of copies sold because of a belief that the author does not understand how percentages of royalties work. There have been instances where authors accused the publisher of "shorting" them when the arithmetic did not multiply out according to the percentage, but this is usually because the author is not aware of sales made at varying prices.

Authors should be assured that most publishers are extremely careful in their accounting methods. The executed contract binds the publisher in a legal responsibility to be totally honest with authors. The author has the legal right to demand an counting of sales and revenue of his book. It is unusual for a publisher not to deal in an honorable fashion with authors. After all a publishing house cannot exist without them.

In summary, the contractual agreement should specify the per cent of royalty due the author, how often it is to be paid, when it is to be paid, and a provision for a statement accounting for the number of copies sold. It is up to the author to see that all of these points are covered in the contract.

Receiving Advance Royalties

Publishers occasionally make advance royalty payments to authors. This may occur if the author has certain expenses in the production of the manuscript, or it may be a publisher's way of assuring an author of the company's belief and faith in the manuscript's potential. Whatever the reason, an author should not be misled into thinking that an advance royalty payment is a bonus or a gift. It is charged against future royalty earnings of the author, and it will be deducted when the first royalty payments are made. If the advance is a particularly large amount, the publisher might arrange a deduction plan that would prorate the payment over a limited number of future royalty payment checks. This method is preferable to having the full advance taken out of the first check. Otherwise, you might receive your first statement printed in red ink, indicating that you owe the publisher until the advance payment is fully reimbursed from sales.

There is one more major item to discuss before concluding "How Do You Negotiate A Contract?" and that is . . .

COAUTHORS—ARE THEY INCLUDED IN THE CONTRACT?

Coauthors are very much a part of the contractual agreement. The publisher is very concerned that every author involved in the manuscript be under contract, regardless of the division of labor. Each author will be issued a contract to sign with his share of the royalty specified.

Division of royalty between two or more authors is their decision. Publishers generally agree to a fixed per cent on a publication regardless of the number of coauthors involved. If two coauthors feel that they have equal contribution to a book bearing a 15 per cent royalty on the hardback edition and agree to a 50–50 share, then each individuals's contract will read "Royalty—7½ per cent." It is not uncommon for an experienced and published author to join with one or more coauthors and have the shares split on a 60–40 basis. Depending upon the contribution, amount of work, and reputation of, for example, five coauthors, the royalty division might be 60–20–10–5–5 per cent of the 15 per cent royalty. This would read in the contract as 9, 3, 1.5, .75, .75 per cent.

Coauthors must fully understand their roles and responsibilities in a joint project. There is the risk that performance and work load might vary from what was anticipated at the time the contractual agreement was signed. Changes in employment may disrupt a writing team, as might a breakdown in the health of one of the members. If a radical departure from the original work load agreement results, it is in order to negotiate a change in the royalty split before the manuscript is completed.

Is it desirable to involve coauthors in your project? Only you can answer that. If you find yourself involved in a work that needs input from others more qualified than you in some particular areas, you should seek additional participants. To what degree you are willing to involve others is your decision. Coauthors might be avoided entirely if an author feels that it would be feasible to hire individuals to produce specific materials for an agreed price and a waiver of any interests in the royalties of the finished product.

The pressure induced by a coauthor agreement can have a very positive effect upon those who are "dreamers" rather than "doers." For every manuscript that has made it successfully to the marketplace, there are thousands still unborn in the brains of "would be" authors because there is a lack of drive to commit the dream to a plan of realization. In many cases, unwillingness to share royalties with others has been the culprit. However, 50 per cent of a publication is far better than 100 per cent of an unfulfilled fantasy! Also, coauthors can exert an influence upon each other that results in a much better product than any one individual might have been able to produce.

Perhaps another reason you have yet to become published is because you have tormented yourself with the question . . .

LITERARY AGENTS—DO YOU NEED ONE?

Literary agents offer many services to authors that you might want to take into consideration. Acting as business agent, they:

1. Advise authors on the marketability of a publication.
2. Represent authors with publishers.
3. Guide authors through contract agreements.
4. Negotiate the best possible royalty payments.

In general, an agent acts upon an author's behalf with the know-how of a professional in a highly competitive market. For such services, an agent gets approximately 15 per cent of an author's royalties.

Authors of textbooks or "how to" books seem less in need of an agent than those writing in the fiction area. Text publishers have a fairly fixed system that deals in a direct method with the author as beneficially as through an agent. Publisher's representatives often act the role of a literary agent, at no cost to the author.

Agents might argue that their services would benefit the author to a greater degree than their fee costs. There are numerous stories regarding authors who never knew success until an agent took them under contract. In contrast, there are just as many tales of successful authors who did not know what to do other than contact the publisher directly. The decision is up to each individual author. If an author has exhausted his known possibilities for getting published, turning to the services of an agent may be the next option.

How do you locate an agent? The quickest source is the advertisements of magazines aimed at writers. You can find them on almost any newsstand and usually in your local library. For example, *Literary Market Place,* a Bowker Company publication, contains a section on agents of all descriptions, and *Writer's Market* devotes many pages to authors' agents. (Further information on agents can be found in Appendix C.)

How do you know if you have selected a reputable literary agent? You don't until you make every effort to check his credentials. You can ask for names of authors the agent has represented, and then contact the authors to see if they were satisfied with his services. You also can find out which publishers the agent deals with, and contact them to verify if this is, in fact, a reputable literary agent whom they would recommend.

A word of caution—working with literary agents is not unlike working with editors. They are experts in their fields, but *you* are an expert in yours. Defend your positions if you believe you are right.

Now that we are about to sign a contractual agreement, have you been asking yourself . . .

DO YOU NEED AN ATTORNEY?

If you do not understand the language of the contract, you probably need an attorney. However, try to avoid one that is going to take on the publishing world and show them what contract law is all about. All you need at this point is to be assured that you have a full understanding of the contractual agreement and that it contains the essential points both you and the publisher agreed to in your initial talks.

Refer to Appendix D to become familiar with a typical contractual agreement. Notice how it is subdivided with headings that make it readily understandable and easily referenced.

If there are sections in the contract you do not agree to, you can cross them out and write in what you do want. Once these changes are initialed by you, you may sign and return the contract to the publisher (see Figure 12). If the publisher agrees to your changes, he will initial them and sign and return your copy of the then legal agreement. If the publisher does not agree to your initialed changes, you may enter further negotiations.

Soon you will go to your mail box and say to yourself, So-o-o-o . . .

```
Mr. B. K. Editor                         February 22, 1977
The Unique Publishing Company
1000 Park Place
Empire City, New York

Dear Mr. Editor:

Enclosed are the signed and initialed copies of the contract
agreement as requested.

Please note that I have indicated a change in the paragraph
concerning the frequency of the payment of the royalty from
annual to semi-annual and have added that a statement of units
of sales will accompany the check.

I feel that this request is not out of line since what I am
asking is almost considered standard procedure between most
publishing houses and their authors.

I am looking forward to receiving your signed copy in the near
future.

                         Sincerely,



                         A. N. Author
                         3078 La Canada Drive
                         Jacksonville, Florida 32216

Enclosures:  2
```

Figure 12
Agreement with Changes

So You Have
A Contract—Now What?

With the preliminaries out of the way and the contract signed, you are now faced with the true test of authorship.

WRITE AND REWRITE

Writing demands self-discipline, so establish a daily routine that includes *at least two hours* to be applied to the material you are trying to produce. Many times you will sit down at the typewriter or with pen in hand thinking that you have nothing to put on papter today. But, as you sit in that writing attitude, you will find yourself putting words on your paper, words you would have missed had you not kept to your routine.

As you write, prepare duplicate material to be kept in separate locations in case one copy is lost of destroyed. The extra work and expense may prove well worth the effort.

Form, Style, and Preparation of the Manuscript

Distinctive form and interesting style are a great stimulus to the sale of every publication. Creative and innovative treatment of the contents can contribute to expanding acceptance in the market. No matter what the form or style might be, however, there are specific recommendations for an author to follow in the preparation of his manuscript.

Your publisher may provide you with a writer's guide. If one is not available to you, this book can serve as a general guide. For more specific and technical information, check your bookstore or local library.

Once you have a professional guide book, use it . . . study it . . . and follow it. Use only one guide book. Don't guess or assume; read your guide until it is familiar to you. Double check it *before* you prepare the editorial copy of your material.

Organization of Chapters

The table of contents you designed for negotiation with the publisher serves now as your guide to writing. Keep it in front of you, and select that chapter you feel most inclined to handle first, whether it is the first, the fifth, or the last.

When you have selected the chapter, study the subheadings you have included and decide which one of them will receive attention today. When that decision has been made, decide how you will break that heading down into other headings (see Figure 13). Notice the slight break in thought in reading the headings in Figure 13. This break occurs because of the differences in word structure. The middle of the list flows well, but another break comes when you get to "Critiques."

WRITING DETAILS

Organization of Chapters
Transitions
Preparing Illustrations
Getting Professional Help
Preparing Final Copy
Critiques (Reviews)
Evaluating Critiques
Rewriting

Figure 13
First List of Headings

```
┌─────────────────────────────────────┐
│         WRITING DETAILS             │
│                                     │
│   Organizing Chapters               │
│   Making Transitions                │
│   Getting Professional Help         │
│   Preparing Illustrations           │
│   Preparing Final Copy              │
│   Obtaining Critiques (Reviews)     │
│   Evaluating Critiques              │
│   Rewriting                         │
└─────────────────────────────────────┘
```

Figure 14
Headings Using Parallelism

This is why professional writing demands parallel structure in headings, so rewrite the headings until you have achieved professional quality (see Figure 14). Compare the reading flow on the two lists of headings and notice how much smoother the Figure 14 headings read. Time spent on such detail establishes the quality level of your work.

When the headings have been properly structured, select the one you wish to discuss first. Write the copy for each heading on a separate page so that they can be shuffled if you later decide that the order of presentation needs to be changed.

Making Transitions

When you have written to each of the headings, and when you are sure that you have them in proper sequence, you must write transitional sentences that allow an easy flow from one paragraph heading to another. When the chapter is finished, read it from beginning to end to make sure that one thought leads naturally into the next and that all relationships are evident.

If illustrative material seems necessary to clarify or picture an idea, make a note in the margin describing the type of illustration needed, such as Figure showing headings, or table or graph showing statistics.

With your first draft, you are concerned only with expressing your thoughts, capturing the essence of your ideas. Once you have done that, you must consider the words you used.

Vocabulary

Words are important because you want your book to be bought and read, and the readers are the ones who will read it and praise it—or put it down and forget it.

Whatever a person's intelligence, reasoning ability, or maturity, whether the book is fiction or a technical manual, chances are that, given a choice between two books on the same subject—one slightly below his reading level and one slightly above, the person will choose the slightly below level. To assure that your writing stays within the reading capability and preference of the audience for which you are writing, use the readability formula in Appendix A before you prepare your final copy. Fry's Readability Chart is simple, reliable, and accepted in the field. This valuable tool will assure you and your publisher that you have kept your writing within the reading level of your proposal.

For example, if you are writing:

1. Romantic Novel—
   the words will be simple, direct, and descriptive (not complex and laden with technical meaning).
2. A Book for Pre-School Children—
   the words will be simple in structure and meaning.
3. A Textbook for Secondary Level—
   technical words, necessary to increase vocabulary, cause readability to rise significantly, so all other words should be easy and selected for interest appeal.

Now would be a good time to study the Evaluative Criteria in Appendix A. Familiarity with what quality is makes it easier to develop quality material.

Illustrations

Illustrations may be used to clarify an idea or to present technical information in a more comprehensible manner than is possible in writing. So, consider carefully any illustration you plan to use.

1. Cartoons—
   can present a concept and break that concept down faster and more effectively than the written word. Many pictures tend to become dated rapidly, but most cartoons age slowly.
2. Tables or Graphs—
   are used to present statistical data. Consider which allows the material to be grasped most effectively. You might want to prepare the illustrations both ways before making your final decision.
3. Color—
   is expensive to print and will increase the cost of the book. For this very basic economic reason, you may be asked by the publisher to use black and white.

   In some manuscripts, however, color can be used to increase the meaning of the illustrations and to make the written content more effective. When that is the case, the price of the book may become less important than the effectiveness of the material included.
4. Narratives and Case Stories—
   are sometimes used to illustrate a concept that is difficult to explain in the usual manner. If they are used, they should portray both the strengths and weaknesses of the characters.

When your first chapter is "cool," look at the marginal notations on illustrations and determine which ones are essential, remembering that they can be added or taken out right up to editorial copy preparation of the manuscript.

Prepare the illustrations yourself if possible, because it is less expensive and you get *exactly* what you want. Even if you hire a local artist or statistician to prepare illustrations, you can supervise their work to obtain the results *you* want. If not, most publishing companies have staff artists or free-lance artists who will turn your ideas into illustrations (in some cases, the cost comes out of your royalties). But remember . . . they are working with a cold idea, and even though you think you are spelling out exactly what you want, the artist's perception may differ from yours.

Prepare each illustration on a separate page. Refer to the publisher's guide for proper formats and for directions to indicate where the illustrations should be included.

When your content and your illustrations have been completed for the chapter, lay it aside. Remember to place one copy in another location where it will be safe. One never expects a catastrophe such as an office fire, but if you are prepared for it, it hurts less.

Polishing Copy

Most writers find that a "cooling off period" is necessary to gain an objective viewpoint on the material just written, so put it aside to "cool." You can start another chapter, and perhaps even finish it, before picking up the first one again.

When your ready to polish your copy, read the chapter as if you had never seen it before. Be critical. You may be surprised at

> awkward sentence structure
> misuse of pronouns
> difficult phrasing.

The best way to find errors is to pretend that the material was written by another person. It's easier to be critical of others than of yourself.

Put the material aside again, and work on other things until you forget, at least to some extent, what you have previously written. Then go through the material again searching for

> precise wording and
> correctness of structure.

The next time you read through the material, count the number of negative statements made. Consider the impact of negative thinking on your readers. Negative statements frequently create defensive thinking on the part of a reader, and may even be considered "condescending" in tone. At the very least, they can be less interesting. Change as many statements as possible to reflect a more positive tone.

An author must write and rewrite—perhaps several times—before he is satisfied with his copy.

Copy Corrections

As you prepare the final copy to be mailed to your publisher, reread your manuscript for correctness. It should be as perfect as you can make it. Think how the headings should look, the type set to be used for certain words or phrases, where the illustrations should be inserted. As you proofread, make corrections above the line at the point of the correction so that they can be easily understood by the typist.

Typing Suggestions

A professional typing job that will create perfect editorial copy is desirable, and even professional typists need basic typing rules to follow. Some common rules are given below for the author's use in making his copy for the typist . . . not to be handed to the typist with the expectation that she spend hours pouring over the rules and the manuscript in total and complete bewilderment.

1. Type all copy double-spaced on white, 8½ × 11, good quality bond paper.
2. Produce 3 sets of your manuscript—one original and one copy for the publisher and one copy for your files (no, your rough draft is not sufficient).

3. Margins are to be set according to your format, but allow at least 1¾″ on all four sides.

4. Page numbers should be typed in the upper right corner of each page of the manuscript, starting with the first page of the text. Include all charts, graphs, and tables through the last page of the appendix. Any pages added after you have completed the numbering should be inserted following the page for which they are intended and given that page number with a small letter designation. For example, if a page is to be added between pages 35 and 36, it would be numbered as page 35a. A notation would be made on page 35 indicating just where 35a should be inserted.

5. Additional pages and/or extensive corrections are to be typed on separate sheets of paper and inserted following the page that notes the inclusion or correction on all copies, as well as on the original (work only with whole sheets—no partial pages, please!)

6. Pages removed from the text are noted by including the number of the removed pages on the previous page. For example, if pages 36, 37 and 38 are removed, the number on page 35 should be changed to read 35-38.

7. Front matter pages (all those preceding page 1 of the text) are numbered consecutively in small roman numerals. The title page is considered the first page, although it will not carry the number i. The next page will carry the number ii, and continue in sequence until the first page of the text is reached.

8. The type bars of the typewriter should be cleaned so they will produce clear, sharp characters. Either a carbon ribbon or a new fabric ribbon should be used so that the type will be dark and consistent throughout the entire manuscript.

Although your major task is the production of the manuscript, there are other things that require your attention.

YOU SUBMIT FINISHED COPY

Check your agreed-upon dates for submission; mark them on your calendar. Publishers work on a production schedule, and any author's delay can be financially costly to them. Production delays also are costly to you, and working well in advance of your deadlines is a good trait to develop.

Sometimes only one deadline is agreed upon—the date for the entire manuscript. If it is agreed that you will mail chapters as they are completed, do so without undue delay. Some publishers like to get several chapters and conduct several evaluations during the manuscript preparation. Be sure you understand the desired procedure.

Checklist for Final Copy

Your final copy should be as complete and correct as you can possibly make it. Reference guides are available at bookstores and libraries. Prentice-Hall, Inc. recommends to its authors the following references:[1]

Spelling *Websters New International Dictionary,* 2nd ed.

Grammatical rules and writing *Handbook for writers,* 3rd ed., Leggett, Mead, Charvat

Language usage *Modern English Usage,* Fowler, or *Usage and Abusage,* Partridge

Writing style *Words Into Type,* Skillins, et al.

To assure you have everything together, the following 15 items should be checked (although some may not apply to every type of publication):

1. *Title Page.* Creating a title for your work was probably one of the first things you did when you conceived your original idea. You should "test" that title at this point. Does it really describe the content as it is completed? If you can improve the title, now is the time.

2. *Dedication Page.* This is not a required item, but if you plan to include one, it can be placed here.

Prentice-Hall Author's Guide (Englewood Cliffs, N.J.: Prentice-Hall, Inc., 1962), pp. 21–22.

3. *Foreword.* The author has the option of including a foreword page. It is usually written by someone other than the author. A survey of other books on the market might help you to decide on its merits.

4. *Preface.* The preface can contribute significantly to the reception of your book if it is written clearly, concisely, and with emphasis on the reader. Brevity in the preface is a virtue—one page is usually sufficient.

5. *Acknowledgments.* Extensive acknowledgments are best treated on a page separate from the preface. Brief acknowledgments may be included at the end of the preface.

6. *Table of Contents.* In Chapter 1 we discussed a tentative Table of Contents. As you finalize your material, you will notice that numerous changes, additions, and/or deletions have taken place in the body of your work. The Contents page now should be restructured to reflect the final copy.

7. *Text.* The final copy stage should find you generally satisfied with the content and its treatment. As a last review, proofread your entire manuscript.

a. Capitalization, punctuation, word choice, and spelling must be correct. You cannot afford to be sensitive about proofreading your material. Tear it apart for accuracy; your future as an author depends on the professional quality of your work.

b. Sentence structure. Are your meanings clear and well stated? Have you avoided verbosity?

c. Watch for misuse of pronouns and check verb tenses.

d. Person and gender. Most technical writing demands the third person structure; however, many textbooks are being written in the second person to increase readability. The material you already have submitted to the publisher was written in the "person" you expect to use, so maintain that style throughout your work. Check carefully to make sure you are not switching back and forth.

e. Check the author's guide for margins, headings, indicating change in type styles, and other format information.

f. Paragraphs. Do your paragraphs demonstrate a continuity of thought? Have you avoided long, rambling, diverse discourses?

Could any paragraph be better understood if broken into two or more paragraphs?

g. Introductions and summaries. Do they actually introduce the subject and summarize it in brief and clear language?

h. Topic Headings. Have you made generous use of topic and subheadings? Could the content be emphasized or clarified with the use of more headings?

i. Vocabulary. Is the vocabulary commensurate to the abilities of the readers for whom the book was written? Have you adequately explained new terminology? Do you need a glossary?

8. *Footnotes.* The treatment of footnotes follows very definite rules that can be found in any of a number of style manuals on the market. The cardinal rule in the use of style manuals is to use only one manual throughout your entire work, and make sure that your references are complete and accurately documented.

9. *Bibliography.* Not all publications need a bibliography. Those that do should be guided by a specific style manual.

10. *Appendices.* Important materials that augment the text, but would be burdensome in the text, are placed in the appendix or appendices.

11. *Glossary.* Terminology that is new but integral to the topic at hand is often best treated in a brief, concise glossary. With a glossary, the reader does not have to explore the text for explanations, and the writer does not fill the text with definitions.

12. *Index.* Publications requiring an index need one that is both complete and well done. A poor job on an index makes a book much less attractive to a buyer. The index cannot be developed until the compositor has pulled the page proofs of the book. Publishing houses handle the index in different ways. An author may have the choice of doing the index himself or he may ask the publisher to engage a professional. If the publisher handles it, the cost may be charged to the author's royalty account.

13. *The End.* The end of the manuscript may be indicated by inserting on the last page the following—# # # or THE END.

14. *File copy*. Make a copy of the final publisher's manuscript for your own safekeeping. Your rough copy will not be sufficient, as you will learn when you get your galley proofs which must be checked against the final manuscript.

15. *Mail the Manuscript*. This is no time to skimp on postage—insure the material and send the original copy by itself first class, registered. This assures you that the publisher received it. Mail it in a flat heavy envelope with a carboard liner. The second copy can follow in the regular mail. By putting them in separate mailings, you increase the odds of at least one copy being received.

Once your manuscript is put in the mail, you wait for . . .

EVALUATION AND FIELD TESTING

To obtain professional critiques, editors often consult various people who work in the field in which you are writing. Excerpts from these reviews may be sent to the author as suggestions or ideas for possible changes in the material.

You may obtain your own critiques if you wish, particularly if you are conducting field tests to validate material. Unless you have a published author among them, it may be unwise to ask for critiques from your friends. You are seeking professional evaluations that will help you prepare material that will sell; your're not—at this point anyway—looking for a pat on the back.

Reviewer's Critiques

Reviewers may raise questions concerning points you may have overlooked or may suggest the inclusion of additional materials. Sometimes certain points of your manuscript need to be explained. You must remember that this is not being done in an argumentative way but in an attempt to improve your publication.

Sometimes reviewers turn in enthusiastic evaluations, but it will be very exceptional if you receive *only* favorable comments and suggestions. A good reviewer will point out weak points, which will help the author strengthen and perfect his work. If a reviewer thinks the manuscript reads like a set of classroom lecture notes, you can expect other readers to respond in the same way. Knowing this gives you the opportunity to consider whether to rewrite for a more polished and professional product.

One of the authors of this book thought that her first writing effort was being reviewed to death. During the preparation of her first manuscript, the publisher changed editors three times. Naturally, each new editor preferred to get a new review of the work, and sent the manuscript out to reviewers. To add to the frustration, the second editor assigned reviewers that were unfamiliar with the subject! The frustrations vanished, however, when the third editor came equipped with expertise in the field and had the material properly evaluated.

Evaluating Critiques

Put aside your personal sensitivity as you read the critical suggestions carefully to determine if you can, or if you want to, incorporate them. If you do, you have no problem. If you do not, you must determine how strongly the editor feels about the suggested changes and, if necessary, about compromising.

It may not happen often, and a beginning author is hardly in a position to become too stubborn, but occasionally this is the point where the editor and the author need to decide if they will mutually agree not to proceed with the publication . . . so be ready to return any advance you may have drawn if you are the one who refuses to change the copy.

Rewriting

Using your copy of the manuscript previously sent to the editor, work the suggested changes into the manuscript. Employ the same technique you used in preparing the original copy:

PROOFREAD AND DOUBLE CHECK

> sentence structure,
> word choice,
> spelling,
> capitalization,
> punctuation.

Make sure that the new material is incorporated so smoothly that it appears to have been there all along. Then, if the changes were extensive, prepare another final copy of the material following the same procedures as before.

Again . . . with a sigh of relief . . . you wait for the time when . . .

YOU CHECK GALLEY PROOFS

When your entire manuscript has been submitted, the editor schedules it for production. You normally will be advised of the anticipated production date. At that time, the production staff has the manuscript set in type as it will appear in print. A limited number of galley proofs are run on very rough paper so that a final check can be made by the author and editor to make sure that any last-minute changes (or corrections) are incorporated before the presses roll to produce the book.

It is not uncommon for galley proofs to have been hand-rolled over the type, thus the expression "pulled galley proofs." The proof is usually on newsprint-grade paper and may be as long as two or three feet; the actual pages may not yet be established.

The purpose of the proof is to check the copy for accuracy against the final manuscript. As the author, you have the privilege of checking the galley proof of your work along with your editor.

Some publishers send the author only one set of galley proofs; others later send a second set called "page proofs." These are proofs of the actual page layout of finished copy.

Whether you are to review one or two sets of proofs, you will be expected to edit them very carefully. This is the author's task—*no one else can do it as effectively as you can.*

Minor changes in this stage of production present little difficulty, but extensive revisions, or the insertion of additional material, may represent extensive changes on the presses. Some publishing houses charge an author for such excessive alterations, particularly on page proofs.

Proofreading

When you receive the galley proofs, you should put everything else aside and give your immediate and concentrated concern to proofreading and material.

1. Compare carefully with your original manuscript.
2. Make sure nothing has been left out.
3. Check illustrations for proper placement.
4. Proofread carefully for technical errors, such as:
   Spelling
   Transposition of words or lines
   Correct word division.

Some standard proofreading marks are shown in Figure 15.

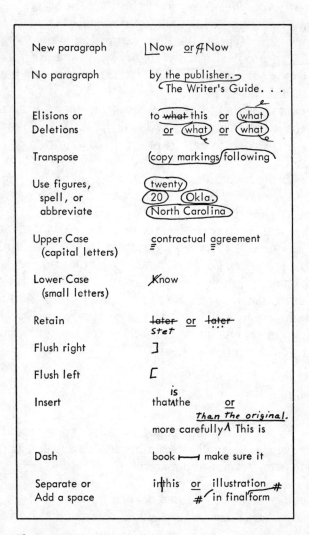

Figure 15
Standard Proofreading Marks

In spite of everyone's best efforts to assure accuracy, errors creep in here and there. The following is a typesetting error that slipped into print:

> There are many different kinds of maps. Some kinds of maps show roads, towns, and Other maps are concerned with the terrain. cities. A familiar example is a road map.

This illustrates the necessity of extreme care and diligence when reading proofs.

Minor changes in copy are relatively inexpensive to make at this point, so your editor will encourage you to make your decisions now rather than at a later stage when it would be more difficult and costly.

Page Proofs

When the production editor sends a second set of proofs, the copy is laid out in page form and may include the illustrations set in the copy as they will appear in final form. These proofs should be checked even more carefully than the original galley proofs, if that is possible. This is the last opportunity for you to make any changes in the copy. Hopefully, you made all of your changes in the previous set of proofs, and the editor has checked for typesetting errors. This is your book . . . make sure it is . . .

THE BEST!!

Once your final proofs are sent back to your editor, you are finally ready to shout . . .

CHAPTER FIVE

Now You're Published! Where's The Bank?

The fantasy of "striking it rich" lies in the heart of every author. Some few have been heard to say, "Oh, no—I'll be pleased just to see my name in print," but let the news of sizable sales become known and the cry will be heard . . . "Where's *my* money?!!"

Over 40,000 books were published last year. Hundreds of thousands of stories, articles, poems, plays, cartoons, and untold other writings were bought by publishers. Unknown millions were written, but never made it to the sales counters of the bookstores or newsstands.

Many authors who do get published suffer the experience of such poor sales of their work that neither they nor their publisher get paid for their efforts. Disappointing? Yes. Disaster? Not necessarily. Publishers often sense the potential of a budding author and will market the first writing, knowing there is a gamble involved. The plan is to break even with the first effort in the hope of success occurring with the second, third, or even the fourth manuscript.

The returns on a highly successful publication can be so great that the venture is often worth the risk involved.

NOVEL WRITING

Best sellers are the ones that appear on the charts in the book sections of Sunday newspapers. Reviewers interview these authors on television shows, and they write about them and their books in nationally syndicated columns. Book clubs compete for the publishing rights of predicted best sellers. Paperback publishing contracts are signed as producers bid for movie rights, and television serialization may lurk in the wings. Authors of these best sellers look for the bank, for it *is* possible to become a millionaire with one such book.

An example of such success is Dennis Smith, author *Report From Engine Co. 82.* The book reviewer in *Tir,* magazine (August 23, 1976) reported how Smith's book became a best seller; then as the paperback and movie contracts were signed, the author was well on the way to becoming a millionaire. Lightening struck twice to author Smith—the market response was so great from the fire fighters in the country that it sparked the idea of starting a monthly magazine for firemen! Smith's *Firehouse* magazine went to press with 50,000 paid subscriptions of $9.60 a year. The first press run was 75,000 copies with 104 pages, of which 54 were paid ads.

ARTICLE AND SHORT STORY WRITING

The success of *Report From Engine Co. 82* is exceptional. There are, however, thousands of writers making an above-average living by writing articles and short stories for newspaper and magazine markets.

Beginning writers usually experience difficulty breaking into the writers' market, but persistence, professional growth, and voluminous writing can produce a five, six, or seven-figure income. Seldom do the thousands of writers published in this market become known nationally. Unless that is very important to you, you may find enough reward in cracking the market and making a good income.

Since one of the big problems for the beginner is learning where to sell his work, Appendix C lists the names of numerous references available to you in libraries and bookstores. The references are in detail, giving the names and addresses of publishers and editors who will look at unsolicited work. In addition, you will find descriptions of the kinds of manuscripts they are buying and how much they will pay.

TEXTBOOK WRITING

The textbook market receives very little publicity, and their sales are not reported in the best seller lists. The potential for authors to make big money in the school book market is far greater, however, than in the novel market.

Millions of textbooks, written on every subject imaginable, are printed every year. Every subject and its educational level is a separate market. The authors of texts must possess a degree of expertise and in-depth knowledge of the field and the particular grade level. Educational levels for these potential markets include:

Preschool	Postgraduate
Kindergarten	Adult education
Elementary school	Special education
Junior high school	Career education
Secondary school	Music and art
Junior college	Vocational
University	Technical
Graduate school	Other specialty

Potential Earnings

A successful junior college textbook with annual sales of 20,000 copies, selling at $12. per copy, can earn, for the author, $20,000 per year. Furthermore, it should go on, year in and year out, if it is kept current through revisions. An elementary textbook that has been adopted by several large populated states can sell hundreds of thousands of copies. *You* figure out the author's possible royalties on that one!

The incredible thing about it all is that once a textbook is published, the royalties can keep coming in for years—just like an annuity. A textbook author was once heard to say: "Finding that royalty check in the mailbox twice a year is just like stumbling over a goldbrick in the middle of the street!"

Well . . . enough dreaming—let's talk about some specifics that confront an author once he is successfully published.

ADVANCES

A major purpose of the advance payment by a publisher is to help the author cover any preparation expenses incurred in the writing of the manuscript. It is reasonable to expect that the author will pay off expenses (typing, secretarial help, copying, illustrating, photos, field testing, or any other item that was a cost in the production of the material).

The advance payment is also extended to assure the author of the publisher's belief and faith in the manuscript. An advance check may be forwarded to the author immediately after the publisher has concluded negotiations, or upon the author's request during manuscript preparation. Remember—this payment is entered in the author's account as a debit, and it will be deducted from royalty checks.

Overpayment of Advances

The advance payment to the author may exceed the amount of actual book earnings, but the author does not have to pay the difference to the publisher. It is the publisher's loss if first edition sales do not reach expectations.

Pressure From an Advance Payment

The publisher gains some leverage over an author through the payment of an advance. It may seem incongruous, but sometimes authors lose the great enthusiasm they demonstrated while putting the publisher's package together, followed by the "headiness" of signing a contract to be published. The grim reality of having to sit down at the typewriter and produce the "great work" does slow some authors down to the point of stagnation—let's face it, we all know of more fun things to do.

Editors have been known to use various kinds of encouragement to dawdling authors, among them the reminder that an advance was made in good faith and the author is expected to perform accordingly. Hopefully, you will be one of those authors who will use the advance payment to produce the manuscript as agreed, and then find that the first royalty check far exceeds the advance.

Which leads us to the next question . . .

ROYALTY CHECKS—ARE THEY GOOD MARKET INDICATORS?

First royalty checks are usually not good indicators of how well your publication is selling. The amount of the check reflects the sales for the period that the book was on the market. Therefore, if your book was on the market for only a month or two before the accounting period closed, the check may not represent an accurate measure of its reception. The first accounting period for some books will reflect a large advance sale to schools and for libraries—a phenomenon that will not usually recur during the life of the book. The second royalty check is a better indicator of how your publication is doing. By the time you receive the third check, you should have a reasonable idea of its salability.

Another area of concern is . . .

PUBLICATION LIFE—HOW TO PROLONG IT

The life of a publication is fairly well defined by its nature. If your manuscript is an article, you know that its publication life probably will be one appearance in the magazine or journal. A book of short stories or a novel could be expected to do well for a year or two at best and then slowly diminish in sales over a period of a few years. Textbooks that become "bibles" in their field can go on selling successfully year after year.

The publication life of texts can be prolonged indefinitely through periodic revisions that keep the material up-dated and fresh. Just the revamping of the cover can revitalize sales. New illustrations, updated photos, or the addition of color can give an old "standard" text a new life, and thus revitalize sales.

The time to consider updating your publication can be indicated by a number of things:

1. Competitors on the market with newer, more up-to-date information then your book offers.
2. A loss of dominance in the market evidenced by a downturn in sales.
3. A change in academic position through new insights of the author.
4. Additional new materials that better compliment the original text.

The author may be more sensitive to the need for revision of a book than the publisher. Being an expert in his field, the author is closer to the needs of the subject area than is the publisher. The publisher has the greater feeling for the marketability of the book. Therefore, it is imperative that a dialogue be maintained between author and publisher so that when the book goes into subsequent editions, the necessary revisions, additions, and rewrites can be effected. Thus the sales can be extended for years to come.

With your book on the market, your attention naturally turns to the question . . .

ROYALTY INCOME—WHAT CAN YOU DO WITH IT—BESIDES SPEND IT?

"Of course I'm going to spend the money! Isn't that what it's for?" is a response often heard from newly published authors. It's a perfectly natural reaction—especially if your life has been one of hard work, hard knocks, and few extra dollars.

But—keep an open mind at this point for there is nothing sadder than an author who blows a fortune, only to find that he is incapable of repeating his writing success. Fortunes are hard to come by, so if you do happen to be among those few who write a really lucrative seller, do some creative planning.

Considerations Affecting a Spending Plan

Your plan to spend your new wealth depends a great deal upon the kind of publication you have sold and how well it is selling. Suppose you sold a novel; its early sales are not bad, but neither are they very good. It was passed over by the book clubs, so you can be fairly sure that it is not going to the top of the best seller list.

Royalties During the First Years.   If the first six months on the market produced sales of 4,500 copies and your royalty is 10 per cent of the retail price of $8, your first royalty check will amount to about $3,600. If sales for the second six months show a 25 per cent increase, but the volume levels off at the year and a half mark, it is time to become realistic. A decrease in sales by the end of the second year is evidence that the book is declining, and it may very well have made the most of its run on the market. Marginal sales may continue for some time, but the initial money returns probably have been realized.

Analysis of Early Royalties. With this novel, you hit a first-year income total of over $8,500. This second year drifted off to about $6,000. The downturn in sales took it to about $3,000 yearly. Depending upon your regular federal income tax bracket, the first-year taxes on the new royalty income could be 20 to 35 per cent—around $2,500. This is a considerable sum of money.

This may not concern you, however. After all, you tell yourself that you're going to get a royalty check every six months, at least for a while. So, you'll have money from later checks to take care of the taxes when they come due.

Problems from Spending the Early Royalties. You might figure that a little spending spree is in order. How about buying a nice new Buick? Not one of the expensive ones—just one that the first year's royalties will cover—say, one that costs about $8,500. The problem this purchase creates is that the whole first year's royalty disappears, and along with it the $2,500 income tax money that should have been set aside for Uncle Sam.

"That's no problem," you may say, 'I'll just cover the taxes with my next six-month royalty check." That might work out, but by that time, another quarterly advance tax payment will confront you. Add this to the first one you deferred and you suddenly find that you have doubled the tax bite, and reduced the spendable amount from the next royalty check by half!!!

Planning Your Spending. Planning for taxes and spending is the only way to enjoy your royalty income. Playing "catch-up" with income taxes is a sure way to get into financial trouble, which can turn the joy of receiving royalties into a nightmare.

This example is fairly conservative. Just imagine if you wrote a successful seller and your annual royalties hit $20,000. Your tax bite would probably exceed $6000!!! How would you ever get out of trouble if you mismanaged your income with taxes running that large?

Uncle Sam Comes First

Before you get into the serious business of spending your
royalties, first figure out what part of the money belongs to the
Internal Revenue Department. We suggest a visit to your local
IRS office where the people are helpful and the service is free.
You also might contact a certified public accountant or a tax
attorney. An hour's time should be sufficient to introduce you
to the responsibilities of your new income tax bracket. This
might involve quarterly advance payments or the setting up of a
reserve fund to cover your new taxes as they come due.

Income Averaging

The quickest and easiest way to reduce your taxes, should
you suddenly make a good deal of money, is to take advantage
of the Income Averaging step allowed on Schedule G of income
tax form 1040. You may average your income over a five-year
period, and you may continue to figure it every year as long as
it is to your advantage to do so.

This helps to reduce the impact of sudden, sizable increases
in your income, and it also helps to soften a sharp reduction as
well. A competent tax consultant can show you how income
averaging can save you tax money, which will leave you with
more "after-tax" money to spend.

But, do you really think you should start to spend yet? Have
you considered . . .

Investment of Royalty Income

Successful authors often become well known in their
communities—particularly by those with propositions designed
to make your royalties grow into two fortunes, one for you and

one for them. Such people include stockbrokers, real estate salesmen, yacht brokers (a yacht is an investment), life insurance representatives, franchisers, benevolent societies, religious groups, "good cause" groups, and the list can go on and on.

If you become one of the fortunate writers who earn a sizable income, the sound judgment you demonstrated in your writing should carry over into your money management. The constant theme throughout books on how to manage money is . . .

spread your risks . . .
and protect your capital.

Cash. You may wish to keep some of your earnings in *cash* in the bank. This may not be spectacular as an investment, but it is available immediately when you need it.

Life Insurance. An adequate *life insurance program* is recommended. What is adequate for you is a personal conclusion, but it seldom will coincide with the recommendations of most life insurance salesmen. Life insurance is *not* an investment. Your insurance plan should have a definite purpose with stated limits. Writers sometimes find it difficult to convince life insurance salesmen that annual royalties become part of an author's estate and will be paid to named beneficiaries, just as life insurance is.

Annual royalties of $20,000 to an estate of a deceased author is like having a quarter of a million dollars of life insurance. A successful author may find that his needs for life insurance are not as great as he might be led to believe.

Then, there are . . .

Tax Sheltered Annuities

The primary purpose of a tax sheltered annuity is to set aside a portion of your income in a prescribed savings plan. The amount saved comes off the top of your income, thus reducing the total income subject to federal income tax. The tax you normally would pay on the saved amount is deferred until you withdraw the savings—ideally in later life when you retire and your income has declined, and you are paying taxes in the lower tax brackets. In this way, you can establish a supplement to Social Security and other retirement plans. An attractive feature to consider is that, of the amount saved, possibly 20 to 30 per cent (which can double every eight or nine years) is actually deferred present tax dollars.

And it is legal! The federal government has set up this plan to encourage private individuals to supplement their personal retirement programs. There are limitations—you are allowed to set aside up to 15 per cent or $7,500 of your annual income, whichever is less.

An author with a sizable income should consult an investment counselor about the numerous plans that are available.

There is also the possibility of investing in . . .

Real Estate

A home is probably one of the best investments you can make. A second home on a lake is also regarded as a pretty good place to put surplus money.

Speculative buying of land or apartment houses? That's a whole new field that will take you out of the "protect your capital" category and put you smack into the "risk" column. This is not to say that you should not consider such opportunities; however, when you consider that your area of expertise is in writing, you need to evaluate the success and failure factors in such a new and different field.

And what about . . .

Stocks

You might invest in *stocks,* which fall into a "risk taking" classification. The market goes up . . . and it goes down! The often quoted saying,

Stocks? It's very easy to make money in stocks. Just buy low and sell high!

If it were all that easy, everyone would be a millionaire. Owning a few shares of stock is good for some snappy conversation at cocktail parties—but most of the brokers are hard pressed to show gains year in and year out that would warrant the risk of your capital!

And what about . . .

Government Bonds, Tax Exempt Municipal Bonds

Here the risk taking is diminished, but so are your returns. At times of inflation, it is difficult to find risk-free investments that can do much more than keep up with the erosion of the dollar. Many advisors feel, however, that if you can do that, you are ahead of the game.

As you can see, the preservation of your money can become a bigger problem than any of those you encountered trying to make it in the first place!

So . . .

Is There a Solution to the Investment Problem?

Perhaps the only solution to the investment problem is to develop a broad program that might include investments of low risk, medium risk, and high risk. No one can come up with the exact answer for you, except you.

J. Paul Getty is reputed to have said that if you had enough money to invest, you should consider investing it in your own business rather than in someone elses!

Now, there's something to think about!

With all that whirling around in your head, are you still wondering . . .

When Do You Get to Spend Some of That Royalty Money?

If your planned spending program concerned itself only with savings and investing, it would make for dull living . . . so allow for some play, like . . .

A three-day weekend once every month!   An expenditure of about $150 per weekend for ten months amounts to only $1500 per year. There's not a marriage (or a relationship) that couldn't benefit from it immensely! And that's worth it right there.

Two weeks in Europe every year!   That will cost $2,500 to $3,500 depending upon how high your tastes run and how imaginative you are in your traveling.

You did agree to plan to spend some of the money on living, didn't you? So . . .

Change Your Routine.   You owe it to yourself to spend at least a portion of this new income for your own form of self-satisfaction. It might range from buying antiques to exploring the world of exotic plants. Whatever it takes, add fun and possibly a new dimension to your daily routine.

There is a special purpose in suggesting changes in your routine. Change brings new energy, new thoughts, and it starts the regenerative processes of your mind. Before long, you'll be eager to face that typewriter again!

While you think about that, let us tantalize you with this thought . . .

SO YOU FINALLY GOT PUBLISHED? IT'S EASIER THE SECOND TIME!

It's easier the second time because you know now that you have what it takes. Self-confidence is a mental elixir; it allows you to proceed with more self-assurance in the preparation of your second manuscript. You've done it once, and you can profit from the mistakes you made the first time. You can be more organized because you realize the need for organization.

It's easier the second time because you know you have the backing of friends and associates who are happy for your first success. Even the ones who show a touch of jealousy give you confidence because you know that they feel you are successful at doing something they would like to do.

It's easier the second time because you can "pace" youself. You know your writing habits, your rate of turning out rough copy, your editing capabilities, your style of putting material together. Therefore, you can budget your time for manuscript preparation with more assurance of meeting deadlines without undue tension and pressure.

It's easier the second time because you know that the finished product will mean more money in your pocket—and that is perhaps the greatest motivation of all to the potential author! With your first book on the market, you can project the market value of your second with greater assurance.

It's easier the second time because you've been published! Whether you approach your first publisher or select a new one, selling your idea is easier the second time simply because you already have been published. This does not mean automatic acceptance, but a publisher will give more serious attention to your propositions because you have shown the capability of producing quality work that sells in the market.

How do you start? As you go through the final stages of your first publication, chances are that you will begin to formulate ideas for your second. Having gone through the experience once you know the procedures for making your second effort a successful venture.

If you are writing in a professional area, you may think of using the professional literature to try out some of your ideas for a second venture. You might decide to write some articles to feel out responses to new thoughts that are emerging in your field.

Sometimes the author of an article will be approached by a publishing company that is in the market for a publication in a particular area. In any event, if your ideas are creative and suggestive, you may hear from a number of people around the country who are impressed with your work. This should encourage you to pursue your propositions. If there are no responses, work up another idea that might be more productive.

Sometimes a new approach is "ahead of its time." That certainly does not mean it should be shelved. Develop the material, polish it, promote the idea through an article in a professional journal. If you receive favorable responses, you may feel the time is right to contact a publisher again.

Reading in your own field, exploring different ideas, propositions, and thoughts of others may show you where new publications are needed. Interviewing practicing professionals about the availability of new or different literature in the field can reveal strengths and weaknesses of existing books, and may help you to generate creative ideas for your next publication.

So, as the ideas begin to surface, start another series of index cards. Write your ideas down, sketchy as they may be. Store them in the file box, adding new ones as they occur. When you are ready to seriously consider starting that second book, your idea file is a ready reference. You may even find that your entire second effort is practically outlined in that file box.

So, you finally got published? Take our word for it—it really is easier the second time!

However it happens . . .

WE WISH YOU THE BEST OF LUCK!!!

APPENDIX A

Evaluative Criteria

The need for critical and objective evaluation of books and publications has led to a concerted effort to develop criteria that is suitable for such evaluation; yet even publishers are far from agreement on the specific essentials to insure the success of a publication. A study of educational literature reveals many commonalities, however, that are important to consider in an evaluation of the content of a book.

Two major aspects of evaluation confront an author:

1. the evaluation of the quality of the content.
2. the equitable treatment (quantity) of major topics.

Consideration of both is necessary for a complete evaluation.

AN EVALUATION FOR QUALITY

The quality of material must reflect the professional level and standards of the field for which it is written. The presentation of material should be in accord with the stated or implied objectives of the author. How well this is done may determine the success of the book or article.

An author can more readily evaluate his writing for quality if he applies specific criteria to major concerns. It should be recognized that, even with a good set of criteria, an evaluation of quality is still somewhat subjective. Every subject area has its own distinctive form and content that may call for slight variations, but careful consideration of each applied against the following criteria will be helpful in assuring high quality content.

To demonstrate an author's use of the criteria, a sample evaluative statement for a hypothetical *Consumer Economics* textbook will follow each criterion.

Professional Level of Material

Criterion 1. Is the reading level of the textbook in accord with the grade level for which it was written?

Reading differs from other forms of communication because the reader controls the rate of assimilation. He can pause to reread a passage, skim rapidly, read slowly, or stop reading altogether. Given a choice between two books on the same topic, one slightly above their reading level and one slightly below, most readers generally will prefer the latter. This is particularly true in textbook selection when one is trying to gain new knowledge. An unnecessarily difficult reading vocabulary may be an obstacle in the path of learning. Readability more nearly can be assured by writing slightly below the level of the projected audience.

There are many reading level formulas available. Fry's Readability Graph[1] is recommended because of its simplicity and usability. Application of this five-step procedure will identify the reading level of your material.

The Reading Ease list (Figure 16) illustrates the five steps. The grid in Figure 17 allows you to plot your reading samples to identify reading level. Three random samples usually are sufficient to identify the overall reading level of a book. Once the samples have been computed (Steps 1-3), find the average number of sentences and the average number of syllables (Step

[1]This graph was published in *The Reading Teacher* (March 1963 and *The Journal of Reading* (April 1968), with Mr. Fry's very gracious release that it be used by anyone if this credit is given.

READING EASE

STEP ONE: Select three 100-word samples. (Stop on 100th word!)

STEP TWO: Count the sentences per sample. (Count the last partial sentence as complete.)

STEP THREE: Count the syllables in the sample. (It is easier to count if the syllables are first marked.)

Sample 1
(A 100-word sample containing 5 sentences and 169 syllables)

[It should not be necessary to master the skills of reading at the	19
same time the reader is gaining new information and ideas. Such	19
obstacles may deter the learner in his formations of under-	18
standings, concepts, and attitudes.	4
In an effort to measure reading ease, readability formulas have	20
been developed. One of the main objections to the use of	19
readability formulas, according to report writing experts, is that	20
too much emphasis on readability by the author takes the art	20
out of writing. Writing will always be an art—and studying the	19
elements of writing which affect readability makes a better	11
artist.] Readability formulas will not provide interest, but they	
do provide a guide for checking writing to see that it is being	
prepared for the right level of audience.	—

Total Syllables = 169

STEP FOUR: Compute the average sentences and syllables from the three samples.

	Samples			
	1	2	3	Averages
Sentences	5	+ 3	+ 3 = 11 ÷ 3	= 3.6
Syllables	169	+ 128	+ 105 = 402 ÷ 3	= 134

STEP FIVE: Plot the position of the text on the Reading Graph by the averages computed.

Example: Vertical axis—sentence average = 3.6
Horizontal axis—syllable average = 134

Reading level = 9th grade

Figure 16
Fry's Readability Graph—Five-Step Procedure

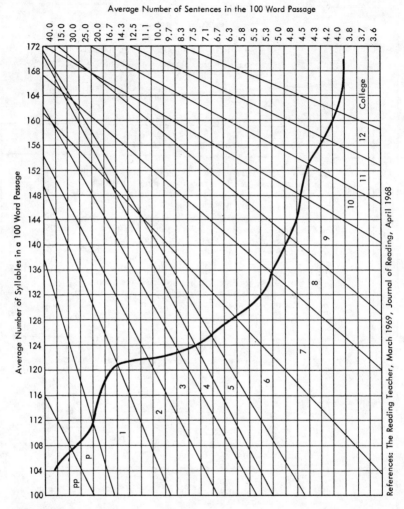

Figure 17
Readability Graph Grid (PP-College)

4). Applying the averages to the grid, most levels will fall near the heavy median line, the reading level lies between the lines identified by the grade level number.

Criterion 2. Does the book develop a vocabulary of specific terms designed to extend the reader's vocabulary?

This criterion is most necessary to any book attempting to provide new information in a specific field. The introduction of new words should be handled so that they can be used with meaning and comprehension. Arbitrary repetition of new words and technical terms should be avoided because it may produce nothing except frustration. However, the ability to think logically and talk intelligently about a subject requires some knowledge of the vocabularly peculiar to that subject.

Criterion 3. Does the author avoid condescension—"talking down" to the reader?

The way an author uses words in sentences is most important to the comprehension of the material. A person "loves" or "hates" a book depending on the effect the words have on his own emotions. Condescension arouses negative emotions, which may interfere with the thinking process. Thus the content of a book may be accurate but unsuccessful. The content should appeal to various senses and be adapted to the interests of potential readers.

Content Emphasis

Criterion 4. Does the book have a sequential curriculum pattern that is most conducive to the learning of the material presented?

Does your treatment of the content present a different and better approach—one that motivates the reader to think? Often this is the very reason why writers feel the need for a new textbook in a particular field. An analysis of the competitive publications on the market should have prompted you to develop an original sequence, which quickly would be recognized as an improvement over existing books, and thus provide a prime reason for acceptance of your material.

Criterion 5. Does the topical emphasis represent a balance that is rational and complementary to the overall subject of the book?

A distortion of the subject can result if the author overemphasizes one area at the expense of others. Sometimes an enthusiasm for a new concept or approach can result in an unbalanced treatment of the total content, causing the book to be unacceptable to other professionals in the field.

Criterion 6. Does the content represent the most recent knowledge available in the field?

A book that fails to include the most recent information pertinent to the subject is instantly out of date, even as it is being published. A serious investigation of the current literature in the field should be evident in the content. Historical findings, archaeological discoveries, and other forms of research are constantly updating the old or creating the new, so it is absolutely necessary that the author be knowledgeable of the most current facts and figures in his field. References to other professional opinions should be noted where there are contrasting viewpoints that could be important in promoting the logical thought processes for the purpose of making decisions or extending comprehension.

Structure of Material

Criterion 7. Does the structure of the material demonstrate the most logical progression through the subject matter?

To be most meaningful to the reader, the material must follow a logical and sequential progression. It should adhere to a step-by-step learning process, with each succeeding step building upon the previous presentation of information.

Criterion 8. Is the progression of subject matter properly recognized and presented in each part of the book (preface, contents, descriptive content, illustrations, end-of-chapter materials, glossary, bibliography, index)?

The reader has a right to know why you designed your particular progression for learning, and the only way he can know is by reading the material in the Preface. If you have a bias, recognize it. If there is a need to overemphasize one area, state the need. Honestly stating your intent allows the reader to put it in proper perspective, and he more readily can perceive your intent and understand your approach. Failure to do so can create misunderstanding and misinterpretation of the actual intent in presenting your material.

Criterion 9. Do the illustrations (both graphic and narrative) add important dimensions to the learning experiences expected from this book?

Pertinent and dramatic illustrations can add tremendous impact to the content of a book. An author should, however, question the relative merits and values of the illustrations. Only the best possible selections should be included. A few illustrations of high quality are preferable to a larger number with doubtful characteristics.

Criterion 10. Does the book have a format that is distinctive, that aids and promotes learning, and that fosters the desire of the reader to explore the entire book?

A writer may produce a book that measures up to all of the aforementioned criteria, yet still find success elusive because little concern was given to the format. Designing a distinctive format calls for creativity, imagination, and inspiration, without which the buyer may see "just another book." Format is the vehicle that can set your creation apart from the competition and can help to make your publication the standard for your area.

EQUITABLE TREATMENT OF MAJOR TOPICS

Equitable treatment of material is measured in terms of the complete presentation, the selection of material, and the total amount of space devoted to each topic. This measurement is purely quantitative, and it is used primarily to determine if each topic received an appropriate amount of attention.

Adequate estimates of the equitable treatment of the major topics in a book can be accomplished only after the author has first formulated a criteria against which to measure the coverage, as evidenced in the preface, contents, descriptive content, illustrations, end-of-chapter materials, glossary, bibliography, and index. Although the following set of criteria was developed to be applied to educational textbooks, writers of other types of publications are encouraged to apply these concepts toward an evaluation of their own work.

Using a hypothetical textbook, *Consumer Economics,* we will assume that the author covered 10 major topics in the book and now wants to measure for equitable coverage. The coverage per cent that each topic received when measured against total coverage of all topics is shown in Figure 17, which demonstrates how the major topic "Money Management" was evaluated. It also compares the coverage of Money Management with the coverage of each of the other nine topics, showing that the heaviest emphasis was given to Money Management. In a consumer economics textbook, this emphasis would be expected.

Criterion 1. To what degree is money management represented in the Preface?

Was a statement included indicating Money Management as a major topic? If so, its importance has been acknowledged. If it is not emphasized, naturally its importance tends to be minimized. Either way, the philosophy of the author is revealed to the reader. The question facing the author at this point of the evaluation is, "What percentage of emphasis on Money Management is evident when compared to the emphasis placed upon the other nine topics?"

Count the total number of words in the Preface. Then count the number of words relating to Money Management, and find the percentage of the total. For the purpose of this example, let us say that 20 per cent was calculated, so this figure was posted under Money Management, Criterion 1 (Figure 18).

Criterion	Money Management	Federal Reserve	Taxation	Supply and Demand	Labor	Government	Distribution	Investments	Economic Theory	Gross National Product	Totals
#1 The Preface	20	10	10	15	7	10	13	10	2	2	100%
#2 Table of Contents	30	5	5	15	10	7	15	5	5	3	100%
#3 Descriptive Content	50	10	10	10	7	5	5	1	1	1	100%
#4 Illustrations	70	--	5	--	5	--	10	8	--	2	100%
#5 End-of-Chapter Materials	70	5	5	--	--	--	5	5	5	5	100%
#6 Glossary Bibliography Index	68	5	5	2	1	2	5	5	5	2	100%

Figure 18

Major Topic Equitable Treatment. This chart demonstrates quantitative coverage for *Consumer Economics*. Notice that the total of 100 per cent is added across the chart for each of the six criteria.

Criterion 2. What is the comparative coverage of Money Management in the headings on the Contents page?

The number of headings that include terminology indicating an emphasis on Money Management are counted. Compared to the total number of topics, a percentage of the equitable treatment for Money Management is obtained—30 per cent was posted to Criterion 2, Money Management (Figure 18).

Criterion 3. What is the comparative extent of the coverage of Money Management in the Descriptive Content?

This measurement can be made only after the rough draft has been completed. The author determines where the emphasis lies, and may even count the number of pages containing Money Management information and take a percentage of the total number of pages in the book. When each topic has been evaluated and the information accumulated, emphasis and biases become evident. The author can then modify, alter, or adjust the treatment of topics more nearly to represent intent. In our example, 50 per cent is posted to Criterion 3, Money Management (Figure 18).

Criterion 4. What is the degree of equitable treatment of Illustrations in the coverage of Money Management?

Graphic illustrations such as pictures, charts, and graphs, or cartoons and narrative illustrations, such as case histories, often are used effectively to supplement the text material. In determining the emphasis on Illustrations in Money Management, a comparative evaluation is made by counting and taking a percentage of total illustrations. In this example, it is found to be 70 per cent and is posted to Criterion 4, Money Management (Figure 18).

Criterion 5. To what extent do End-of-Chapter Materials emphasize Money Management?

End-of-Chapter Materials that promote development and experience beyond the textbook must be evaluated; 70 per cent is entered on the chart for Criterion 5, Money Management (Figure 18).

Criterion 6. What is the extent of treatment of Money Management in the Glossary, Bibliography, and Index? (These are included together because usually a textbook will have one of the three, but not necessarily all.)

It is important to determine the quantitative emphasis on specific areas, whether it is to provide vocabulary development, references for additional reading, or indication of where specific material may be located. Therefore, terms, references, and indexed terms should be counted and the comparative percentages figured. In this case, Glossary, Bibliography, and Index, as applied to Money Management, was determined to be 68 per cent and was posted to Criterion 6 (Figure 18).

Analysis of Figure 18

Figure 18 should be regarded as a guide. There may be many areas with which an author is entirely satisfied, even though the percentages indicate an out-of-balance emphasis—this is a prerogative of being an author. Criterion 3, Descriptive Content, is the key to the entire evaluation. Once the author is satisfied with the degrees of emphasis among the major topics, everything else can be evaluated relative to that emphasis. It can be readily observed in Figure 18, however, that numerous percentages show extreme differences, indicating a need for extensive revisions.

For example, Money Management is indicated by Criterion 3, Descriptive Content, as the primary subject of the entire work. However, the figures in Criteria 1 and 2 do not reflect this. If the author is satisfied with the Descriptive Content, this would indicate that additional emphasis should be written into the Preface and Contents to represent the subject in a better way. The figures for Criteria 4, 5, and 6 indicate a possible *over*emphasis of Money Management. The author should interpret this as an indication to review and reevaluate these areas—it could be that he is entirely satisfied with the ratio as it is, but it may be that this has alerted the author to the need for alteration of the overemphasis.

Assume that Descriptive Content (3) in Figure 18 is acceptable to the author as a fairly accurate representation of his work—what changes would you recommend? Circle those figures you find to be out of balance with Criterion **3**. As an author, you are now faced with the decision of what to do about it.

Once you have completed your own evaluation, you may notice areas you would like to compare with what other authors have done in the field. This same application of criteria can be performed on any textbook in the same manner and then can be compared. Be supercritical of your own work. You are doing these evaluations to make your own work better, not to pat yourself on the back. Pats on the back can come after you begin receiving the royalty checks.

These criteria were developed from a more extensive work prepared as part of a doctoral dissertation.[2] The dissertation was much more detailed on the research into each topic and provided a more detailed breakdown of criterions. Some authors may be interested in pursuing the evaluation in greater depth, but we feel those presented here are adequate for most purposes.

[2]Loras Evelyn Vancil Brunson, *An Evaluation of Secondary School Business Textbook Coverage of Money Management* (Norman, Ok.: University of Oklahoma, Graduate Dissertation, 1965).

A Sample Contractual Agreement

A sample of a fairly typical agreement is included for the benefit of those writers who have yet to sign such a contract.

If the authors of this book had been aware of the information available in this text and had actually read such a sample contract prior to signing for their respective first books, they would have been prepared to negotiate more favorable contracts.

It is hoped that as a result of this book, your negotiations with future publishers will bring about the most favorable terms possible.

A MEMORANDUM OF AGREEMENT made on this _____ day in the month of _____ 19__ between _____ (Author) _____ and _____ (Publisher)

IT IS HEREBY AGREED BY THE AUTHOR AND PUBLISHER THAT:

The Authors convey to the Publisher the rights to print, publish and sell a manuscript of the following description—_____, hereinafter refered to as the Work under the following conditions:

Declaration of Ownership

1. The Work is the exclusive property of the Authors and they have the rights to sell, convey and grant to the Publisher the exclusive right to copyright, publish and sell the Work.

Author's Guarantee

2. The Author guarantees that the Work violates no existing copyright, contains nothing of a liblous nature, nor has been previously published.

3. The Publisher will be held harmless from any damages, fees and/or expenses and will be indemnified by the Authors for any such claims based upon copyright infringement, libel or any other claim against the content of the Work.

Manuscript Submission

4. The Author will forward to the Publisher two copies of the completed and revised manuscript on or before (date stated.) Included shall be the index, drawings, maps, photographs, or other materials ready for reproduction. In the event such materials are not provided or are not of satisfactory quality the Publisher will do the work and assess the costs from any sums due the Author from royalties accrued.

Author's Royalties

5. The Publisher will manufacture and sell the Work at its own expense and will pay the Author a royalty based upon actual cash received by the Publisher, of:

___% of paperback editions
___% of hardcover editions

Payment of Royalties

6. The Publisher will pay the Author accrued royalties on a semi-annual basis in June and December based upon the report of sales ending the prior March 31 and September 30. (If coauthors are involved each is here named with the agreed per cent of the royalty assigned)

Author's Copies

7. The Author shall be provided (10) copies of the Work at no cost. Additional copies may be purchased by the Author at wholesale cost.

Title of Work

8. The Publisher reserves the right to change or alter the title of the Work as it deems necessary.

Editing

9. The Publisher shall be the sole judge of the Work, edit and determine the form and nature of the publication.

Figure 19

A Sample Contractual Agreement

Publishing Details

10. The Publisher shall publish and market the Work as it deems fitting and shall maintain exclusive control of its manufacture and distribution.

11. The Work will be published on or before the ___ day of the month of _____ 19__. The Author shall have the right to reclaim the Work if this date is not met, in which case this agreement shall be considered terminated.

Proof Changes

12. The Author will correct and change the proofs of the Work. Alterations of proofs, other than printers' errors after corrections have been carried out by the compositors will be charged to the Author's royalty account.

Revisions or New Editions

13. Revision of the Work is hereby agreed to by the Author. Should the Author fail to do so within a reasonable time after the request the Publisher may arrange for such editorial work and deduct reasonable costs from any sums due the Author. Should the Publisher desire revisions or new editions after the death or disability of the Author the costs of such work will be charged to the Author's royalty account and those who performed the work shall be credited in the revised Work or later edition.

Renewal of Copyright

14. The Author agrees to renew the copyright of the Work and assign to the Publisher the exclusive rights as for the original copyright term.

Ancillary Rights of The Publisher

15. The Publisher shall have the exclusive right to sell to others the right to publish special editions of the Work. Proceeds from such sale or sales shall be divided with the Author on a 50/50 basis.

16. The Publisher shall have the exclusive right to sell the rights for use by television, radio, screen or stage. In lieu of royalties the net compensation shall be divided ¾ to the Author and ¼ to the Publisher.

17. The Publisher shall have the exclusive right to sell the right to reproduce all or part of the Work for filmstrips, sound recording and any other method. The net proceeds from such sales shall be divided equally between the Author and the Publisher.

18. The Publisher shall have the right to sell the Work for special edition by a book club or other organization. The lump sum shall be equally divided between the Author and the Publisher.

19. The Publisher shall have the right to sell the Work on a royalty basis in countries outside of the United States. In such case the royalty shall be equally divided between the Author and the Publisher.

20. The Publisher shall have the right to sell in quantity to schoolbook depositories, school districts, educational associations and others with the agreed understanding that the Author's royalty shall be (a lesser) percent.

Discontinuance of Publication

21. When the market for the Work no longer justifies its manufacture, the Authors will be so notified in writing by the Publisher. The Authors shall have a period of thirty days thereafter in which to exercise the right to buy from the Publisher all copies on hand at one half of the wholesale price, thereafter this agreement shall cease and terminate.

Figure 19
Continued

Conflict of Interest

22. The Author shall not print or have published any material or work that would be deemed by the Publisher in conflict with the sale of the published Work.

Subsequent Work

23. The Publisher shall be given by the Author the option for publication of any subsequent work of a like or similar kind of material.

The content of this agreement shall be binding upon the Author, heirs, executors, successors, and assignees during the term of the life of the publication, copyright, and renewal thereof.

DATE _____ 19____

AUTHOR SIGNATURE   PUBLISHER SIGNATURE

_____   _____

_____   _____
        Witness

_____
        Witness

Figure 19
Continued

Market References

Do you want to know what publisher is interested in the kind of material you are writing? How much will they pay? What is their address? What is the name of the editor to contact? Where can you locate an agent? Do you need the services of an experienced artist? Do you want an editorial review of your manuscript, the resources of a photo library? Do you want to know of the literary prizes available? What does the international market have to offer? What do you do with ideas for greeting cards? What magazines are interested in humor material? Do you want to join a writers' organization?

The answers to these and thousands of other questions regarding writing, publishing, and marketing of every kind of material are available at your nearest library.

Most local public libraries have at least some of the reference books discussed in this appendix. Libraries in large towns and cities, in colleges and universities will have all the references discussed here, and others besides. Most writers exhibit great surprise when they first encounter this "gold mine" of information. To many it has been the best kept secret in the world! The information is all at the library—free for the asking. And what's more, a gentle request will turn most librarians into veritable dynamos of action surrounding you with references stacked on top of references—and a smile of appreciation is all that's asked for!

HOW TO EXPLORE THE MARKET

Bowker Publications

Among the most valuable sources available to a writer at the library are the numerous references produced by R.R. Bowker Company, Inc., a Xerox Education Company, 1180 Avenue of the Americas, New York, New York 10036. The primary source is *Books in Print*—four volumes (two volumes listed by author, two volumes listed by title). This source lists over 450,000 titles available from some 3,800 publishers. It lists authors, titles, publishers, and prices.

Bowker has subdivided the *Books in Print* series and also has added other publications according to the following interest areas:

1. *Subject Guide to Books In Print*
2. *Children's Books in Print*
3. *Paperbound Books in Print*
3. *Medical Books in Print*
5. *Business Books in Print*
6. *Scientific and Technical Books in Print*

Each source lists author, title, publisher, and price.

You will appreciate the value of these resource books on your very first search. As an example, suppose you went on a camping trip, and, upon your return, you decide that since you have so many humorous experiences to relate you want to draw a cartoon joke book. Who would publish such a book?

An investigation of *Subject Guide to Books in Print* will reveal books published under the following headings:

1. Camping (99 listings)
2. Jokes—See Wit and Humor
3. Wit and Humor (approximately 300 listings)

4. Psychology (29 listings)
5. Pictoral (26 listings)
6. Caricatures and Cartoons (approximately 150 listings)
7. Cartoonists (6 listings)
8. Comic Books, Strips, and such (approximately 90 listings)

Under each heading are numerous titles of books already on the market. The investigation would lead you to identify the publishers who do publish materials in these areas.

Armed with this information, you can then go to Bowker's six-volume series, *The Publishers' Trade List Annual.* There you will be able to determine the relative size of the firm, other titles published, and the address.

In a matter of minutes, you can identify your objectives and decide how to pursue them.

The editors of *Books In Print* do not include publications other than books, such as periodicals, puzzles, calendars, microforms, or audiovisual materials.

Annually in the spring, a *Books in Print Supplement* is published giving price changes, titles that have gone out-of-print, and new books published or announced following the publication of *Books In Print.*

R. R. Bowker Company also publishes *Forthcoming Books,* a bimonthly publication that provides author-title indexes to all books due to appear in the coming five-month period. Since forecasts may be incomplete, inaccurate, or unfulfilled, the *Weekly Record* lists new books actually published.

El-Hi Textbooks in Print gives a more comprehensive list of textbooks for elementary and secondary schools; *Law Books In Print,* published by Glanville Publishers, Inc., covers a good deal not to be found in *Books In Print.*

Subject Guide to Books In Print follows the headings assigned by the Library of Congress. Fiction is omitted unless it is extensive and authentic enough to warrant mention, poetry and drama are omitted; juvenile fiction is usually omitted but juvenile nonfiction is represented. Bibles, as such, are omitted, although commentaries, histories, and versions other than the standard English are extensively covered.

Subject Guide headings are arranged alphabetically, and many of the main entries are further broken down:

Accounting—Dictionaries
Accounting—Examinations, Questions
Accounting—Law
Accounting—Problems, Exercises

The headings are explicit rather than general. Thus books on cost accounting are under cost accounting, not under accounting. Books on actors and actresses are under actors and actresses, not under theater. The *Subject Guide* lists books where the user will be most likely to look for them.

Children's Books In Print includes some 39,000 titles available from almost 700 United States publishers. It provides an author index, an alphabetically arranged title index, and an alphabetically arranged index of illustrators. A list of the book publishers appears at the end of the reference.

Following are other valuable references produced by Bowker.

Literary Market Place

This is one of the most comprehensive resources available to a writer. Listed below is the subject arrangement.

Book Publishing
   U.S. Book Publishers (with three classified sections: 1. geographically, 2. fields of activity, 3. subject matter); Micro publishers; Publishers' Sales Representatives; Canadian Book Publishers; Adult Book Clubs; Juvenile Book Clubs

Associations
   Book Trade and Allied Associations; Literary and Writers' Associations; Advertising, Magazine, and Press Associations; Motion Picture, Music, Radio, and Television Associations; National Associations

Book Trade Events
Calendar of Book Trade and Promotional Events; Literary Awards

Courses, Conferences, and Contests
Courses for the Book Trade; Writers' Conferences; Prize Contests Open; Literary Fellowships and Grants

Agents and Agencies
Authors' Agents; U.S. Agents of Foreign Publishers; Illustration Agents; Lecture Agents; Advertising Agencies; Employment Agencies; Government Agencies; International Agencies; Foundations

Services and Suppliers:
Consulting and Editorial Services (classified by service offered); Data Processing Services; Public Relations Services; Research Organizations; Clipping Bureaus; Free-Lance Editorial Work; Steno and Typing Services; Translators (classified by languages); Artists and Art Services; Artists' Supplies; Photographers; Photo Services; Photo and Picture Sources; Messenger Services; Shipping Services; Shipping Suppliers

Direct Mail Promotion
Direct Mail Specialists; Advertising, Printing and Allied Services; Lettershop, Duplicating, and Mailing Services; Mailing Lists

Review, Selection, and Reference
Book Review Services; Book Review Syndicates; Columnists and Commentators; Adult Book Lists and Catalogs; Juvenile Book Lists and Catalogs; Exhibits; Reference Books of the Trade

Radio, Television, and Motion Pictures
Major Networks; Local Stations; Educational Television; Radio Programs Featuring Books; Television Programs Featuring Books. Juvenile Programs—Radio and Television; Motion Picture Companies and Independent Producers

Wholesale, Export and Import
Wholesalers to Bookstores; Wholesalers in Special Subjects; Wholesalers to schools and Libraries; Prebinders to Schools and Libraries; Wholesale Remainder Dealers; Exporters and Importers; Export Representatives

Book Manufacturing
Book Manufacturers (classified by services offered); Hand Bookbinders; Binders Dies; Cover Boards; Bookbinding Supplies; Book Paper Merchants; Book Paper Mills; Type Manufacturers

Magazine and Newspaper Publishing
Magazines (classified by subject matter); Magazine Subscription Agencies; Subscription Fulfillment Companies; Newspapers; Newspapers—New York Representatives; Newspaper Magazine Sections; News Services and Feature Syndicates

Names and Numbers

American Book Trade Directory, 22nd edition

Booksellers and Antiquarians in the United States, Puerto Rico, and Regions Administered by the United States
United States, Pacific Islands, Puerto Rico, and Virgin Islands

Wholesalers of Books and Magazines in the United States and Canada
Wholesalers; National Distributors of Paperbacks; Wholesale Remainder Dealers

Book Trade Information
Auctioneers of Literary Property; Appraisers of Library Collections; Dealers in Foreign Language Books; Bookstores Classified by Language; Export Representatives; Exporters; Importers; Greeting Card Publishers; Private Book Clubs; Rental Library Chains

Publishers in the United States
Directory of Book Publishers; Publishers' Imprints; Affiliated Companies; Subsidiaries and Special Distribution Arrangements; Former Publishing Companies Now Inactive, Out of Business, or Merged

Book Trade in Canada, Great Britain, and the Republic of Ireland
Booksellers in Canada; Booksellers in Great Britain; Booksellers in the Republic of Ireland; Publishers in Canada; Publishers in Great Britain; American Representatives of British Publishers; British Representatives of American Publishers; Publishers in the Republic of Ireland

Index to Booksellers and Wholesalers in the United States and Canada

International Literary Market Place

Annually reviews the book publishing business at the international level, from Algeria to Zambia.

International Book Publishers
Producers and Distributors of Nonprint Materials
Publishers' Representatives and Literary Agents
Book Clubs
Book Trade Organizations
Calendar of Book Trade, Film, and Related Events
1976 Holidays
Bibliography of Book Trade Reference Sources
Periodicals Reviewing Foreign Language Films
Foreign Literary Periodicals
International Literary Prizes
The United Nations and Some of its Agencies
Export-Import Information
Mailing Information

Magazines for Libraries, 2nd edition

An index by subject of every magazine published.

Aeronautics and Space Science
Africa
Aging
Agriculture
Anthropology
Archaeology
Architecture
Art
Astrology
Astronomy
Atmospheric Sciences
Automobiles
    General; Motorcycles; Special and Technical; Trailers
Bibliography
Biological Sciences
    General; Biochemistry and Biophysics; Botany; Genetics;
    Microbiology; Physiology; Zoology
Blacks
Books and Book Reviews
Business
    General; Accounting and Taxation; Advertising, and
    Marketing; Banking and Finance; Commerce, Industry,
    and Trade; Investments; Management, Administration,
    and Personnel
Chemistry
Children
    For children; About Children
China and Asia
City Magazines
Civil Liberties
Comics
    Magazines about Comics; Boys and Girls; Elementary and
    Junior High; Young Women, Adventure and Romance;

Costumed Heros; Westerns; War; Weird Fantasy; Fantasy
Adventure; Foreign Language
Communications and Media
Computers and Automation
Consumer Services
Counterculture
Alternative Living; Local and Political Change;
Underground Comix; Underground Newspapers
Criminology and Law Enforcement
Cultural-Social Studies
Dance
Earth Sciences
Economics
Education
General; Counterculture; Elementary and Secondary
Education; Higher Education
Engineering and Technology
General; Chemical; Civil; Electrical; Mechanical
Environment and Conservation—
General; Camping; Mountaineering and Trails; Or-
nithology; Special Interest
Environmental Sciences
Europe and Middle East
English Language General; French Language; German
Language; Italian Language
Fiction
General; Science Fiction
Folklore
Foreign Language Teaching
Free Magazines
Games
Gardening
Genealogy and Heraldry
General Magazines
Geography
Government Magazines
Guides and Indexes; United States; United Nations and
Selected Foreign

Health
  General; Counterculture; Drugs
History
  General American and Canadian; States and Provinces
Hobbies
  Antiques and Collecting; Arts and Crafts; Numismatics;
  Philately; Models
Home Economics
Horses
Humor
Indians (American)
  General; Newspapers and Bulletins
Interior Design
Journalism and Writing
  Journalism; Journalism Reviews; Writing and Com-
  munications
Labor and Industrial Relations
Latin American and Chicano
  English; General; Chicano; Spanish; American Magazines
  in Spanish
Law
Library Periodicals
Linguistics and Philology
Literary Reviews
Literature
  General; Author Newsletters and Journals
Little Magazines
Mathematics
Medical Sciences
  General; Nursing
Men's Magazines
Military
Motion Pictures
  General; Fan Magazines; Foreign Language; Professional;
  Reviews
Music
  General; Counterculture; Folk, Rock, and Jazz; Record
  and Tape Reviews

News and Opinion Magazines
    General; Political Opinion Reviews; Radical Right;
    Radical Left
Newspapers
    U.S. National; International; Special Interest; Newspaper
    Indexes
Oceanography
Occult and Witchcraft
Occupations and Employment
Parapsychology
Peace
Pets
Philosophy
Photography
Physics
Poetry
    Little Magazine Genre; Traditional Academic
Political Science
Psychology
Radio, Television, and Electronics
Religion and Theology
    General; Denominations; Secular; Counterculture
Science
Sociology
    General; Social Service and Welfare
Sports
    General; Boats and Boating; Fishing, Hunting, and Guns;
    Physical Education and School Sports
Theater
Travel and Regional
    General Travel; State and Regional
Urban Studies
USSR and East Europe
    English Language General; Slavic Language; Emigre
    Magazines
Wine Magazines
Women and Teen-Age
    General; Women's Liberation; Teen-Age

Paperbound Books in Print, 1977

Contains more than 140,000 titles; gives title, author, and some 450 subject indexes. It deals with the following basic subjects:

Art
Biography
Business
Cooking
Crafts
Drama
Education
Fiction
Games
History
Humor
Juvenile
Language
Literature
Medicine
Music
Nature
Philosophy
Poetry
Political Science
Psychology
Reference
Religion
Science
Sociology
Travel

Publishers' Trade List Annual

This collection of publishers' catalogs is arranged alphabetically by publishers' names and is bound into several volumes each year. The amount of information varies, ranging from full information to short title and price. An alphabetical list of the publishers included is given in the first volume.

Publishers Weekly

Publishers Weekly is the recognized weekly trade journal of the industry. It covers trade news, business forecasts, and lists weekly best sellers. As an example of its coverage, the issue of July 26, 1976, Vol. 210, No. 4 includes:

Media
The Week
People
Rights and Permissions
Economic Review of the Book Industry
Trade News
Forecasts
    Fiction, Nonfiction, Paperbacks, Children's Books
Weekly Exchange
Paperback Best Sellers
Hardcover Best Sellers

Other Reference Materials

1. Marquis Academic Media, a division of Marquis Who's Who, Inc., Chicago, Illinois, provides the academic and professional communities with information on the expanding range of journals and new titles opening in specialized and scholarly fields in their publication, *Directory of Publishing Opportunities.*

It includes more than 2,600 specialized and professional journals. Entries are arranged within 69 specific fields of interest. Only those periodicals are included that represent real publishing opportunities and accept submissions in English. General interest publications have been avoided. Listed are

those with special interests aimed at a limited section of the
public, trade journals, professional magazines, technical journals, and publications produced by business firms, unions, or
associations. The contents include:

Humanities
Interdisciplinary and Area Studies
Social Studies
Communications
Education
Geography
History
Law and Public Administrative
Military
Political Science
Psychology and Mental Health
Social Welfare
Sociology and Anthropology
Women's Studies
Science and Technology
Earth Science
Engineering and Allied Sciences
Environment and Conservation
Life Sciences
Physical Sciences
Mathematics
Medicine and Medical Sciences
Trades, Manufacturing, and Industry

2. *The Writer's Digest* (9933 Alliance Rd., Cincinnati, Ohio
45242) is a monthly magazine directed to writers and writers'
markets in feature stories. It includes:

The Writing Life
The Market Update
Poetry
Nonfiction
Cartooning
The Markets
Contests and Awards

Letters
Books

3. Also published by *Writer's Digest* is *Writer's Market,* primarily aimed at free-lance writers. The contents of the 1976 edition include:

Free lance at Work
   Writing—To Be Read; Finding Your Market; Selling Short Fiction; Selling Magazine Articles; Selling Photographs; Publishing Poetry; Selling Fillers; Selling Your Book; The Market for Plays; Selling TV Scripts; "Breaking In" to Any Market; Sidelines; Preparing Manuscripts; Covering Letters; Mailing Manuscripts; Waiting . . . How Long?; Rejections—Not Death Certificates; Copyright; The "Rights" You Sell; Your Freedom as a Writer
   How Much Should I Charge?
   Selling Pictures With Your Words
Consumer Publications
   Alternative; Animal; Art; Association, Club, and Fraternal; Astrology and Psychic; Automotive and Motorcycle; Aviation; Black; Business and Finance; Child Care and Parental Guidance; College, University, and Alumni; Comic Book Publications; Confession; Consumer Service and Business Opportunity; Detective and Crime; Education; Food and Drink; General Interest; Photography; Plastics, Plumbing, Heating, Air Conditioning, and Refrigeration; Power and Power Plants; Printing; Railroad; Real Estate; Recreation Park and Campground Management; Secretarial; Selling and Merchandising; Show People and Amusements; Sport Trade; Stone and Quarry Products; Textile; Toy, Novelty, and Hobby; Trailers; Transportation; Travel; Veterinary; Water Supply and Sewage Disposal
Book Publishers
Subsidy Book Publishers
Miscellaneous Free-lance Markets and Services
   Audiovisual Markets; Authors' Agents; Contests and Awards; Gag and Humor Markets; Government Informa-

tion Sources; Greeting Card Publishers; Play Producers;
Play Publishers; Syndicates; Writers' Clubs; Writers' Con-
ferences; Writers' Organizations
Foreign Markets
Consumer Publications; Trade, Technical, and Profes-
sional Journals; Book Publishers; Syndicates
Picture Sources

4. A. Bruce Hartung (Box 71, Dallas, N.C.) publishes *A
Writer's Guide to Journals in Education,* which is designed to
aid the educator in identifying some 150 journals and preparing
manuscripts for submision. It provides such information as
editor, address of publication, circulation, frequency of issue,
field or fields of specialization, and other information. The
distributor is Wallace-Homestead, Des Moines, Iowa.

SAMPLE OF BOOK PUBLISHER'S CATALOG OFFERINGS

The review of the publications produced by the few
publishing firms listed here is just a sample of the thousands
that are on the market. This information is available from each
company's catalog. Bookstores, company sales people, and
representatives all have copies of these catalogs. However, the
most accessible source is at the library. As discussed earlier,
consult the six-volume collection of publisher's catalogs, *The
Publisher's Trade List Annual.* This excellent source identifies
who is and—equally important—who is not publishing in a certain field. A visit to the bookstores will reveal the kind and style
of publications that a particular publisher produces.

Equipped with this necessary information, you are ready to
polish your publisher's package and make contact with the
publisher of your choice.

Addison-Wesley Publishing Company, Inc.
2725 Sand Hill Road, Menlo Park, California 94025

The Higher Education Group
Advanced Book Program
Science and Mathematics Division

> Social Science and Humanities Division
> Business and Professional Division
> Cummings Publishing Company, Inc.
> W. A. Benjamin, Inc.

The Juvenile Division
  Addisonian Press
  Young Scott Books

Arco Publishing Company, Inc.
219 Park Avenue South, New York, New York 10003
  Includes the following books distributed by Arco, Arc, United States Naval Institute, Len Morgan, Aerofact, and Pagurian Press.

Animals
Antiques
Arms, Armor, Military, and Ships
Arts
Astrology, Handwriting, Hypnosis, Occult Arts, Palmistry
Automotive
Aviation
Business—Career
Children's Books
Civil Service
Cookery
Crafts, Hobbies, and Games
Do-It-Yourself
English Language
Foreign Languages
Gardening—Flowers
Health and Fitness
H.S. and College Preparation
History
Horse Books
Junior Science and Math
Law and Police Science
Literature
Medicine
Military Exams

Miscellaneous
Pagurian Press Books
Professional Career Exam Series
Science and Technology
Self-Improvement and Study aids
Sports and Physical Education
Teacher License
Teacher Materials
Test Preparation—General
Travel and Adventure
United States Naval Institute Books
Women's Interest

The Bobbs-Merrill Company, Inc. and Howard W. Sams & Co., Inc.
4300 West 62nd Street, Indianapolis, Indiana 46268

The Bobbs-Merrill Company, Inc.:
Law Division
　Law and Law School Books by author
　Law and Law School Books by title
Education Division
　Educational Textbooks
　Odyssey Press
Trade Division
　Adult Trade Books by author
　Juvenile Trade Books by title
　Trade Books by title
Childhood of Famous Americans Series
　Childhood of Famous Americans Series by title
College Division
　College Books and Textbooks by author
　College Books and Textbooks by title
Howard W. Sams & Co., Inc.:
Technical Books
Educational Materials
　Arts, Vocational, Technical
　Business, Hospitality, Fashion

Audel Books
Editors and Engineers Books

Thomas Y. Crowell Company, Inc.
666 Fifth Avenue, New York, New York 10019

Adult Trade Books
Books for Children and Young People
Crowell Peperbacks for Children
Reference books
Audiovisual Materials
Apollo Editions (Crowell titles)
College Textbooks

Doubleday & Company, Inc.
245 Park Avenue, New York, New York 10017

Anthologies and Collections
Biography and Memoirs
Business and Economics
Child Care and Education
Fine Arts
   Arts and Architecture
   Art (self-instruction)
   Dance
   Music
   Theatre and Film
Food and Drink
Foreign Languages
Health and Medicine
   General
   Diet
History
   General
   Mainstream of America Sries
   Mainstream of the Modern World Series
   Zenith Books
Home and Homemaking
   General
   Decorating

Gardening
Sewing
Humor
Mysticism and the Occult
Natural Science
   General
   American Museum Science Books
   Anchor Natural History and Natural History Library
   Doubleday Nature Guides
   Natural History Press
   North American Nature Series
Poetry
Politics and Current Affairs
Recreation
   Crafts, Games, Hobbies, Pets, Sports
Reference
   Basic and General
   College Course Guides
   Made Simple Books
   Tutor Texts
   Writing and Speaking
Religion
   Catholic
   Protestant and General
   Inspirational
Science and Mathematics
   General
   Science Study Series
Social Sciences: Anthropology, Archaeology, Philosophy,
   Psychology, Sociology
   American Museum Sourcebooks in Anthropology
Travel
   Guides, Picture Books
   Personal Travel

E.P. Dutton & Co., Inc.
201 Park Avenue South, New York, New York 10003
   Adult Paperbacks
   Anytime Books

Children's Illustrated Classics
Dutton Lifetime Library Bindings
Dutton Paperbacks
Dutton/Cista Paperbacks
Everyman's Library American Edition
Everyman's Paperbacks
Richard W. Baron Publishing Co., Inc.
Bradbury Press, Inc.
The Chatham Press, Inc.
Arthur Fields Books, Inc.
Liveright
Nash Publishing Corporation
Reader's Digest Press
Riverwood Publishers Ltd.
Saturday Review Press
Sunrise Books
Windmill Books

Harcourt Brace Jovanovich, Inc.
757 Third Avenue, New York, New York, 10017

Elementary and Secondary School Materials

The School Department—textbooks, teacher's manuals, tests, workbooks, filmstrips, tapes, records, and classroom laboratories.

The Center for the Study of Instruction (CSI) conducts research in curriculum and produces school learning materials.

The division of Urban Education (DUE) publishes learning materials related to the definable needs of children in straitened environments.

Guidance Associates produces audiovisual materials in guidance, literature, social studies, and elementary school curriculum.

Beckley-Cardy Company.

College and Professional Books and Journals

The College Department publishes textbooks, workbooks, teaching tests, and audiovisual materials for college and university courses.

Academic Press, Inc. publishes scientific and humanistic books and journals as well as college textbooks.

Johnson Reprint Corporation publishes facsimile reprint editions of scholarly works.

Media Systems Corporation produces audiovisual materials for community colleges.

Grune & Stratton, Inc. publishes books in medicine and psychology.

Standardized Tests and Testing Services
The Test Department creates and publishes tests designed to assess abilities, aptitudes, and learning achievement. Provides testing services and scoring and processing of test results.

The Psychological Corporation applies psychological measurement to functions of industry, government, and education.

General Books
The Trade Department publishes books of general and popular interest, both hardback and paperback, by American and foreign authors.

McGraw-Hill Book Company
1221 Avenue of the Americas, New York, New York 10020

Gregg Division
Shorthand; Typewriting; Office Education; Accounting; Data Processing and Computing; Distributive Education; Other Business Education; Vocational Services

Community College Division
Study Skills; Data Processing and Computer Programming; Civil Technology; Electrical and Electronics Technology; Mathematics, Science, and English; Mechanical Technology; Automotive Technology; Human Service Occupations; Business and Management

College Division
Multicore; AudioVisual; Business and Economics; Engineering; Science; Social Science and Humanities; Medical; Dentistry; Nursing; Allied Health

Professional and Reference
   Technical Books; Encyclopedia of World Art; Dictionary
   on Scientific and Technical Terms; Dictionary of Art;
   Book Clubs; Encyclopedia of World Biography; General
   Reference Books; Business Books; Mail Order Courses

Legal Publications
Paperbacks
Trade—General
Scholarly Books Program
Gregg Instructional Aids

Webster
   Spelling; Foreign Language; Social Studies; Elementary
   Language Arts; Home Economics and Guidance; Early
   Childhood Educations; Health and Safety; Industrial
   Education; Secondary Language Arts; Mathematics
   Laboaratory Materials; Sullivan Titles

National Learning Corporation
DuPont Street, Plainview, New York 11803

Basic Education
Career Education
Vocational-Technical Education
City, State, and Federal Jobs
Teacher Certification
College and Professional School Admission
Graduate School Matriculation
High School and College Equivalency
External Degree Programs
Professional Licensure in Medicine, Law, Real Estate
Library, Nursing, Technology, and others

Civil Service Examinations (CSE)
Teachers' License Examinations (TLE)
National Teacher Examinations (NTE)
Admission Test Series (ATS)
Graduate Record Examination Series (GRE)
College Level Examination Series (CLEP)
College Proficiency Examination Series (CPEP)

Regents External Degree Series (REDP)
Merriwell Series (FM)

Prentice-Hall, Inc.
Englewood Cliffs, New Jersey 07632

School Textbooks
College Textbooks
Reference—Texts
Professional Education Books
Encyclopedias, Business Books, and Executive Reports
Spectrum Paperbacks
Trade and Adult
Children's Books
Children's Paperbacks
General Interest Paperbacks
Dictionaries
Medical (ACC)
Nursing (ACC)

W. B. Saunders Company
West Washington Square, Philadelphia, Pennsylvania 19105

Medicine
Surgery
Dentistry
Nursing
Biology
Chemistry
Mathematics
Physics
Psychology
Business Education
Health
Physical Education
Veterinary Medicine

SCHOOL LIBRARY BOOK COLLECTIONS

An author should have some awareness and knowledge of the
publications in his interest area that are already on the market.

An investigation can avoid duplication of content and/or repetition of titles already published.

The following references specialize in recommended school library and textbook collections at various school levels. A review of these sources can give an author much insight as to what is (and is not) recommended. Publishers names and addresses are listed as well as authors, titles, and prices.

This kind of information can facilitate your crossreference investigation, can help you to identify the need for your publication, and can aid in locating a publisher.

Elementary. The Bro-Dart Foundation, New Brunswick, New Jersey. This source defines a library collection suitable for elementary schools. The references are coded to indicate interest appeal as well as reading levels. Reading levels for grades one and two are based on the Spache formula; other levels are based on the Fry Graph for Estimating Readability. It provides a listing of audiovisual materials that should be in the library to supplement the books.

Junior High School. H.W. Wilson Co., New York, New York. This catalog is designed to support the curriculum of a good junior high school, and the second edition includes nearly 3,500 titles and more than 8,800 analytical entries appropriate for grades seven through nine. It is divided into three parts:

Part 1—The classified catalog is arranged according to the Abridged Dewey Decimal Classification with complete bibliographical information for each book.
Part 2—Author, title, subject, and analytical index.
Part 3—Directory of publishers and distributors.

High School. H.W. Wilson Co. The classified catalog is arranged with nonfiction books first, classified by the Dewey Decimal Classification, followed by the fiction books, followed by the short story collection.

Books for Junior College Libraries. American Library Association, Chicago, Illinois. This source contains nearly

20,000 titles selected primarily for the transfer or liberal arts programs. It does not attempt to cover the areas of terminal and vocational courses offered.

Books for College Libraries. American Library Association. This reference lists titles nearly 39,000 with a bias toward the liberal arts.

NEWSPAPERS, MAGAZINES, AND TRADE PUBLICATIONS

The *Ayer Directory* (Ayer Press, West Washington Square, Philadelphia, Pennsylvania 19106) provides facts about virtually every kind of publication originating in the United States, its territories, Canada, Bermuda, and the republics of Panama and the Philippines. It is widely used as the basic authority by professionals in business, industry, education, publicity and public relations, agriculture, religion, government, and advertising. The directory includes:

Map Locations—towns and cities listed alphabetically with symbols that correspond to map locations
County Seats
Census Figures
Alphabetical Arrangement of Publications. In each city and town, newspapers are listed in alphabetical order by their distinctive names.
Statistical Data

A *Directory of Publishers* is published by The National Association of College Stores, Oberlin, Ohio 44074. It contains an alphabetical listing of publishers and addresses.

Index